THE ANATOMY OF
AFRICAN MISERY

THE ANATOMY OF
AFRICAN MISERY

LORD OLIVIER

"TIME LONGER DAN ROPE"
(West Indian Slave Proverb)

The Black Heritage Library Collection

BOOKS FOR LIBRARIES PRESS
FREEPORT, NEW YORK
1972

First Published 1927
Reprinted 1972

Reprinted from a copy in the
Fisk University Library Negro Collection

INTERNATIONAL STANDARD BOOK NUMBER:
0-8369-8984-8

LIBRARY OF CONGRESS CATALOG CARD NUMBER:
74-38017

PRINTED IN THE UNITED STATES OF AMERICA
BY
NEW WORLD BOOK MANUFACTURING CO., INC.
HALLANDALE, FLORIDA 33009

CONTENTS

CHAP.   PAGE

I. THE SLAVERY MATRIX 7

II. THE INHERITANCE 14

III. CAPITALISM REINFORCES . . . 26

IV. FAFNIR INCUBATES 31

V. THE APPLE OF DISCORD . . . 40

VI. INFECTION TRAVELS NORTH . . . 46

VII. CAPITALIST IMPERIALISM . . . 60

VIII. SEGREGATION 68

IX. AFRIKANDERUS CONTRA MUNDUM . . 85

X. THE LAND GRIEVANCE 94

XI. GENERAL HERTZOG'S EIRENICON TO THE NATIVE 104

XII. LAND AND THE POOR WHITE . . 119

XIII. RACIAL DISCRIMINATION . . . 128

XIV. COLOUR WAR 141

XV. ANTI-INDIANISM 153

XVI. SOME SOUTH AFRICAN WITNESSES . . 160

XVII. THE CONVERSION OF KENYA . . 178

XVIII. AFRIKANDER PROVINCIALISM . . . 191

XIX. THE FIVE FEARS OF SOUTH AFRICA . 208

XX. CONCLUSIONS 227

NOTE. AFRICAN CAPACITY AND CHARACTER 233

5

Dedicated to my SOUTH AFRICAN
COUSINS, of the family of JOURDAIN
D'OLIVIER, of Amsterdam, Diamond
Merchant, sometime Pastor of the Re-
formed Protestant Religion at Pau
in the Pyrenees, and of Nay, in Béarn,
France, exile for spiritual liberty.

THE ANATOMY OF
AFRICAN MISERY

CHAPTER I

THE SLAVERY MATRIX

THE coast of Florida, on whose beaches Western
civilisation appears destined to culminate, was
the scene of the first enterprise of European
colonisation in North America. Before the end
of the sixteenth century the Spaniards had there
imported, as they had also into the West Indies,
negro slaves, to perform for white invaders the
plantation and menial work which the natives
could not be compelled or induced to submit to.
The colony of Virginia was founded by the
London Company in 1607. In 1619 there was
instituted there the first democratic legislature
established by Europeans in North America; and
in the same year the first importation of negro
slaves was bought from a Dutch trader. In 1718
the state of Louisiana was founded, under
Law's Mississippi Company, with 1500 colonists.
Next year 500 West African negroes were supplied
to set up plantations. In 1721, 1000 more

colonists entered, and were equipped with 1367 more negro slaves. By 1790, when the first census of the United States was taken, the total population was under four millions, of whom 700,000 were negroes—more than half a million in slavery.

The Dutch East India Company founded their Colony of the Cape of Good Hope in 1652. The first settlers included Hollanders, Germans, Flemings, Poles, and Portuguese, who are described in the *Encyclopædia Britannica* as having been "for the most part people of low station and indifferent character, with a small number of a higher class, from whom was selected a Council to assist the Governor."

The Company proceeded to import Malays as slaves (from Java) and negroes (from East and West Africa). Its directors, who intended the settlement to be used to produce revenue for their shareholders, prescribed the crops to be grown, levied toll of produce, and harassed the settlers with other exactions. Their monopolist policy first engendered the tendency of the less tractable settlers to move away out of reach of the Company's control, a process to which the first effective obstacle was met with in Bantu tribes, who were encountered east of the Gamtoo River, and pushed back as far as the Fish River. The Hottentots of the Cape had already been destroyed, driven away, enslaved, or subdued.

In 1716 the Dutch East India Company inquired of the local Council whether it would be

8

more advantageous to employ European labour than slaves. Only two members voted for white labour. The comments of the Company's representative, von Imhof, show that the foundations of the South African civilisation of to-day were then already well and truly laid. He explained that:

"Having imported slaves . . . every common or ordinary European becomes a gentleman, and prefers to be served rather than to serve. We have in addition the fact that the majority of the farmers are not farmers in the real sense of the word, but plantation owners, and many of them consider it a shame to work with their own hands."

In 1795 the Colony revolted from Holland. The Cape was occupied by a British force, restored to Holland, reconquered in 1806, and finally ceded to Britain in 1815. The British dealt with the Bantu in a series of "Kaffir wars," and from 1820 onward introduced British immigrants, founding Grahamstown and Port Elizabeth in the Eastern Province. In 1834 slavery was, by the British Government, made illegal, and the slaves were declared free. The labour system on which the farming industry of the Colony had been built up was disorganised. The compensation promised by the British Government was whittled down to about one-third of the valuation of the slaves and even this was in many cases not paid. Great numbers of the Boers sold their farms for what they would fetch, and trekked as pastoral settlers, some north of the Orange River and some into Natal. Their leader, Pieter Retief, in their manifesto disowning allegiance to the British flag, declared on behalf of the emigrants:

> "We are resolved . . . to uphold the first principles of liberty; but while we shall take care that no one shall be held in a state of slavery, it is our determination to maintain such regulations as shall . . . procure the proper relations between master and servant."

This determination their descendants maintain to this day in the Masters and Servants Laws of their Provinces. Illustrations of what are still considered throughout South Africa "proper relations" will transpire incidentally in later parts of this book.

British interests in India demanded that British control should be maintained over the Cape and adjacent territories. The Christian missionaries and the Liberal politicians at that period in power at home favoured the policy of developing South Africa as a group of states under native rule and missionary guidance. The Boers were headed off in Natal by British annexation, and retired across the Drakensberg. The Orange River Territory was annexed in 1848, and the Boer Independents trekked north of the Vaal River. Four years later the attempt to maintain British authority beyond the Vaal was abandoned and the Boers were formally absolved from allegiance by treaty. In 1854 the claim of British sovereignty over the Orange River Territory was also relinquished and the Republic of the Orange Free State set up. The constitution of the South African (Transvaal) Republic declared that "the people is determined to permit no equality between white and black, in Church or State." The Orange Free State maintained the same policy, and the Apprenticeship Laws assigned a status of "tutelage" to all natives that could be made amenable to it. The provisions of the Land Bill now proposed by General Hertzog's Government will, as I shall presently point out, reinforce, if passed into law, this system of native bondage.

I have indicated the coincidence that the foundations of the slave civilisations of both the United States and South Africa were laid by European joint stock capitalist companies who sent out the European settlers and provided the slaves for their use. The method of these colonisations was a deliberate process addressed to the purpose of investing European capital at a profit, on territory appropriated without regard to any rights of natives of the annexed countries. Any resistance on their part was dealt with as savage treachery, justifying extermination. It is not probable that the early settlers at the Cape could have established a slave civilisation there out of native material, any more than the Spaniards could in Florida, the English in Virginia and their adjacent colonies, or the French in Louisiana. If the Cape Colonists could have done so the Dutch East India Company would not have imported negroes and Malays. Not until the settlement was established, and its economy and white militia forces organised, was it possible for its members to capture and enslave Hottentots and incorporate them in their plantation and domestic system.

The Spaniards, through the agency of Sir John Hawkins (whose native industrial genius first conceived this fruitful idea), and of other British gentlemen adventurers and piratical Dutch traders of the period, had introduced West African negro slaves, forcibly kidnapped, into the New World plantations because the invaders were not able to use the native "Indians," who were either killed in fighting, or where there was a hinterland, ran away, or, if reduced to servitude, as they were in Jamaica and other manageable-sized islands, died out. Africans were tougher material. Negro slavery was therefore approved by the charitably-minded of those times as doubly blessed: it introduced the African to the boons of civilisation and Christianity, and it delayed the extermination of the Arawak and the Indian.

Slavery was not necessary for the white colonisation of either North America or South Africa. They were countries of great fertility and delightful climate, where white men could have done their own work and produced, as they have done, a vigorous breed of people. Alien slaves were introduced in order that profit might be made by European capitalists and British and Dutch slave traders. White convicts, later, were recognised to be quite suitable as labourers for the plantations, and were allotted as bondsmen and bondswomen to the planters. Neglected by economic historians, the memory of this class is kept green by fiction in the names of Manon L'Escaut and Moll Flanders.

CHAPTER II

THE INHERITANCE

In the year 1925 a Commission was appointed by the Government of South Africa "to consider the effects of different wage and labour policies upon the opportunities of employment at a wage compatible with a civilised standard of life." This Commission presented, in February 1926, two reports, the signatories being equally divided, three and three. There is a certain degree of divergence between the views of the two sections as to future labour policy, principally turning on the question of the importation of native labour from outside the Union to meet the demands of the mining industry. As to the originating causes of the present economic and social difficulties, both sections are in practical agreement, though the Left Wing Report brings out some of those causes with greater clearness and emphasis; and one member corrects the crudities of his colleagues' idea of the State by long quotations from the writings of Friedrich Engels.

The Commissioners, even of the more Conservative section, emphasise what they describe as: ". . . the gravity of the permanent influences of a nature peculiar to South Africa, that aggravate the position." These are summed up in the phrase: "The Poor White Problem." The so-called Poor Whites, they say, "chiefly represent the failures of agriculture. While in some cases the failure is probably due to personal defects of character or ability, in the main it is due to circumstances over which the victims could exercise no control. However caused, economic failures in agriculture drove the countryman to the town, where the lack of any specialised training for urban occupations and the inability to adapt himself to the different circumstances of urban life inevitably led to unemployment or intermittent unemployment, with consequent economic and personal deterioration."

An underlying cause, they state, "of this situation exists in the unusual circumstances of agricultural tenure in South Africa. White labourers for wages or salaries are few in number. So are tenants at a money rent: instead, there is a class which partakes of the character both of employee and tenant—called in South Africa 'bywoners'—(by-dwellers)." The original Boer farm unit was about ten square miles of country: the normal unit is still from 1500 acres upwards; but many of the older farms have now been much cut up and many congested by common owner-ships of numerous family shareholders. The bywoner, then, is a landless man, allowed to reside on a farm, growing food crops and keeping stock for his own support, often with some help from the owner, while the owner secures, without any disbursement of cash, white assistants without whom he would be wholly dependent on native or coloured labour. There are also some natives and coloured people occupying land on similar terms. The bywoner has no security of tenure or status. The transition from an extensive pastoral farming to agriculture or intensive stock-raising shoulders him off the improving farmer's land. The growth of population in the older settled districts adds to the landless class, whilst the accommodation for them as bywoners diminishes. The Boer War, and the collapse of agricultural values shortly after the Great War, drove many off the land who never recovered their footing; every season rendered unprofitable by drought, hail, excessive rain, stock diseases, locusts or other plagues, detaches another swarm of bywoners and drives them towards the towns. Poor Whites are estimated as numbering from eight to ten per cent. of the white population, say, for a mean, 130,000.

This description by the Commissioners of a phenomenon which they speak of as peculiar to South Africa will not sound unfamiliar to historical or economic students. The tenant for labour service on large estates, driven off after various vicissitudes in his tenure and status to suit the improving economy of the landlord, or by the collapse of his own business, is one of the best remembered figures in English social history. His evolution gave birth to our Poor Law.

The speciality in the fate of the South African bywoner is not his position as a tenant by service, and his ejection, in due course, from such tenancy —these have been common features of all private property large-estate land systems—its distinction is due to the survival in South Africa of the determination of white men to use black men as slaves. It lies in the circumstances in which the South African bywoner finds himself after he is thrust off the land, namely, that neither in agricultural nor manufacturing industry can he find re-employment at wages on which he can live at the minimum white man's standard. The institution of slavery, which was deliberately and without economic necessity made the basis of the original economy of the Cape Colony, is primarily responsible for discrimination between the humanity of the white and the black races, and derivatively for the monstrous and diseased development which that discrimination has grown into among whites in South Africa, approached only—as a result of cognate causes—but not equalled, in the southern United States. This is admitted and unquestioned by all reflective commentators on the history of South African social conditions. The Economic Commissioners recognise it as a truism. They quote expositions, for example: "Generally speaking," the Director of the South African Census wrote in his last Report, "in many, if not all walks of life, there has been a pronounced tendency to regard it as beneath the dignity of a white person to perform menial tasks. This departure from the traditions in Europe of the original settlers in the country is attributed by historians to the importation of slaves into the Cape in 1658, which is stated to have had, in the direction indicated, an important effect on the industrial and social history of the Colony. Slavery brought manual labour into contempt, and the result was that the Colonists ceased to do heavy manual labour. The introduction of slaves was regarded as having had a baneful effect on the industrial history of the settlement. Theal (the historian of South Africa) remarks: 'The system of negro slavery caused the Colonists to regard the black man as properly the hewer of wood and drawer of water.' This idea once started has become, with the passage of time, long after the abolition of slavery, a deep-rooted characteristic of the South African people, and is doubtless responsible in great measure for the increasing number of Poor Whites whose existence constitutes one of the most serious problems of the Union."

Other causes, unquestionably, have contributed to race prejudice, and to the prevailing Afrikander conviction of the necessity for keeping the native in what is considered his proper place. The trekking Boers had to fight desperately for their lives against Bantu tribes, and narrowly escaped extermination by treacherous massacre. They were conscious that the natives who surrounded them, or with whom they contested the occupation of the lands they invaded, had, like the Hottentot servants whom they claimed the right to discipline in their own methods, some sympathy from

British missionaries, who asserted the human rights of liberty and equality, and also of British Imperialism, which pursued them doggedly, if intermittently, with its encirclement policy, in Natal, Zululand, Basutoland, Swaziland (incidentally grabbing the diamond district of Kimberley out of the Orange Free State), and completing the process by the precipitate annexation of Eastern Bechuanaland, to head them off from the Cape to Cairo route on that side, and of Matabeleland to block them permanently on the north; after which the *coup de grâce* (incautiously and prematurely anticipated by the Jameson Raid) could be given to their independence by the Boer War. The Boers, if they were to hold their own as Republics, could not afford to deal with Bantu, Bushmen, or Hottentots except by teaching them that the man with firearms was master of the man with the knob-kerry, the assegai, or the poisoned arrow; and this necessity co-operated with the old slave-state morality to establish their repudiation of the views of the missionaries and of British Liberalism. On the other hand, in their pastoral solitudes they became divorced from the habit of earlier generations of white settlers of freely stultifying any colour-bar doctrine by those irregular unions with female natives from which nearly half a million of the Cape population descend, including the specifically designated community of the Bastaards. On the High Veld early marriages were universal. Bantu women were inaccessible, and the preponderantly female white community jealously enforced domesticity. The Boer Sarahs were fertile. The Reformed Church, whilst quoting "cursed be Canaan" in justification of dealings with natives, disallowed the equally scriptural precedent of Hagar. This taboo checked mixed breeding and accentuated the division between white and black.

The matured and combined result of this economic and political history has been to establish throughout South Africa, but most uncompromisingly in the Bantu lands outside of the Cape Province, colonised by the Boers, a discrimination between white man's status and Kaffir status—and, correspondingly, white man's work and Kaffir's work—the latter including all unskilled manual labour. The white man commands, directs, supervises; the black man works. Further, the employer in all classes, acting in accordance with the essential principles of capitalist economics, has consistently taken advantage of the cheapness of the subsistence needs of the Kaffir, of his ignorance of the ways of white civilisation and of his political impotence to keep down the wages of all unskilled labour to levels at which the white man cannot live on them. Agriculture predominated, and in other nascent industries it could not be permitted that wages should tempt black labour away from the farms.

Even before the Cape Boers were deprived, through emancipation, of servile black or coloured plantation labour, they were betaking themselves to a predominantly pastoral system, which enabled them largely to dispense with it. As long as there was plenty of room for expansion they scattered, and whenever new land was required they trekked farther north. Food was easily obtained, as game was plentiful, and a very little planting and sowing produced enough corn, vegetables and fruit for the family needs. There was no production for sale, for there was no market. There was very little currency or need for it. Hence arose the custom of compounding for service in kind—"the rationing system"—and the impossibility of any white wage-earning class being developed. The white bywoner might do some manual work, handle cattle or drive transport, but it was work for himself or a neighbour and not for wages. When the Boer communities were sufficiently well established to apply themselves to more settled farming, and sufficiently well organised to compel the northern natives to work for them, or be driven away, they invariably paid their wages chiefly if not wholly in kind. To-day, agricultural wages for natives may be put at, on the average, 15s. to 20s. a month (often less) with rations, a hut (made by the native), and some privileges on the farm.

The modern history of South Africa (says Theal) may be regarded as beginning in 1873. Up to fifty years ago the community maintained this primitive or patriarchal semi-servile economy. With the discovery of diamonds and gold, the capitalist régime was introduced. As soon as diamond-getting began to be capitalised, the industry demanded manual wage-workers. The landless whites of the country, unskilled, but held back by the taboo against manual labour, even those who had started as miners, preferred to sell out their claims and (except as prospectors and "river-diggers," each driving a Kaffir boy or two) kept out of the new industries, which were capitalised and developed on the basis of low-paid non-European labour. Engineering and other skilled European labour was imported at very high wages. The theory took root unquestioned and became firmly established that low-paid native workers had to be the basis of the mining industry, and that there was no place in it for white men in any but the higher skilled posts.

When therefore, now, the prolific agricultural class has pullulated the landless white man, and he is thrust off from the halfway perch of the bywoner, he finds himself in a position in which the only work he has had the slightest chance of learning—farm labour—is both tabooed for him because it is Kaffir's work, and also impossible for him because he cannot live on Kaffir's wages.

Great numbers of the Poor Whites are illiterate, or at best very ignorant and ill-educated. They had a bad start: the difficulties of education in their scattered farmsteads were enormous. Great efforts have been made, and with creditable success, to improve matters; but we find them still spoken of by other whites as the most barbarous part of the whole South African population. They are usually only fit for unskilled manual industrial work. From this they are also debarred by the same conditions as debar them from agricultural wage labour.

Twenty years ago the Transvaal Indigency Commission (1906–8) reported that the prejudice against unskilled labour, as being Kaffir work, lay at the root of the Poor White difficulty. The Commissioners of 1925 assert the same. And the ban of unemployment remains unmitigated, because the Kaffir's wage is kept low by the land monopoly and the industrial laws and customs of White South Africa, with the assistance of the Portuguese labour laws over the border.

It is conceivable, though improbable, that if manufacturing and technical industry had developed gradually in South Africa, out of and subsidiary to the more primitive pastoral and agricultural civilisation, the Poor Whites thrust off from the land might have found employment in such new industries, as the surplus of the rural population did in this country. The fundamental obstacle of prejudice against "Kaffir work" on the part of the bywoner, which had no effectual parallel among the indigent workers in England, might conceivably have been circumvented had the industries grown up from small individualist origins and not been started as capitalist enterprises demanding large batches of wage-workers. No such evolution occurred. Only in the Cape Colony coloured, as distinguished from native, employees earn good wages as artisans and trade-labourers as they do in the British West Indies, because they were not denied education by their dominant kinsfolk.

Capitalised industrial production on the plantation and factory system made its first conspicuous appearance in South Africa in the Natal sugar industry. So far as the internal economy of that industry was concerned, there was no more reason why it should not have been developed entirely with white labour, than there was, later, in Queensland, where, after beginning with imported "Kanaka" labour from the Pacific Islands, the white wage-workers, having political power, determined that it should be a white man's industry, paying white man's wages, and proved this possible. High Protection would have been necessary—but there would have been no local difficulty about that. Not only, however, was there no white working class in Natal seeking employment, but the notion of plantation labour, and the unskilled work of a sugar factory, being done by white workers was entirely repugnant to South African social theory. Fortunately, at that period, in Natal, the idea of forced native labour was also repugnant to the British authorities and the colonists. The educational value for the native of compulsory work under any casual white man had not yet been philosophised by Mr Benjamin Kidd, nor its necessity as a basis for British colonisation in Kenya preached by Lord Delamere. Voluntary Kaffir labour, even

24

if it had been available, not being efficient or docile enough for plantation work, indentured Indian coolies were introduced, and the tradition of racial work and racial pay, the work untouchable by a white man, the pay far below what the white man needed to live on, was maintained and re-inforced. The skilled workers required were imported, from Mauritius or England. This Indian immigration not only reinforced the block of low-paid non-European labour in agriculture which the white agricultural community in South Africa had already built up against the future of its own offspring, but gave birth to a new block of like character in the staffing and garrisoning by the intelligent, industrious, and adaptable Indian community of distributive and minor technical productive services which, in the natural development of a prosperous white community, not parasitic on coloured labour, would have afforded remunerative employment to whites. The anti-Asiatic political campaign in Natal is directed chiefly against the competition of Indians in retail trade and in semi-skilled industries, such as painting, carpentering, and cheap tailoring, which no white Afrikander, when Indians were first introduced, desired to soil his fingers with. And the campaign even now appears to be actuated less by South African-bred white men than by British and other European or Levantine immigrants and their descendants.

CHAPTER III

THE causes, then, which were preparing for the South African Poor White class, when it should, in due course, inevitably make its appearance, an impossible situation, originated in the introduction of slave labour by the Dutch East India Company, and were reduplicated and made permanently operative in Natal and reinforced throughout South Africa by the deliberate importation and establishment of a parallel system of capitalist development by underpaid bond labour, the issue of which is a population of about 150,000 Indians established on a basis of earnings and livelihood at which the Poor White cannot live, except at the cost of becoming a human trash much more worthless and unprofitable than either the Zulu or the Indian. This was brought about by British capitalist and employing enterprise in a British Crown Colony. Afrikanderism was not responsible for it; indeed protested against it; and the Colony of Natal, as soon as it could control its own affairs, adopted a vindictive and persecuting policy towards Indians, which led the Indian Government to suspend indentured migration. Later the Government of Natal stopped all Indian immigration altogether. But the effects remain, consolidating and buttressing the block

26

against the normal development of white civilisation throughout South Africa, and form an exasperating element among the present problems of the Dominion.

For the transplanted Indian, and the large population which he has bred in Natal, is more than a passive obstacle, as the Kaffir is, to the employment of the white in unskilled occupations. By his industry and capacity in agriculture and gardening he has established a large area of prosperous intensive cultivation in the hot coast-belt of Natal. In that art he has no rival, and as a purveyor of fruit and vegetables to the towns no white man can compete with him. Nor, indeed, is there much jealousy of him on this score, among or on behalf of the Poor Whites. But he has overstepped the bounds of Kaffir work and is establishing himself at wages in trades which have been regarded as the prerogative of the white in Natal and the Boer provinces, and of the coloured and white in the Cape Colony: building trade work, especially painting, joinery, furniture making, shoe-making, and notably tailoring. Most of all he has established himself as a retail trader in all departments. When the indentured coolies were introduced, Moslem traders and pedlars came with them, and were welcomed as a necessary class for supplying the coolies' needs. These traders prospered and extended their trade to the natives, whose requirements they met more cleverly and cheaply than the white shopkeepers. The native is a

fanciful customer; the Indian appreciates his
right to exercise taste and studies his desires.
The white retailer merely thinks he is perverse
and does not know what is good for him. It is
complained that Indian retailers are making it
impossible for white men to live by shopkeeping:
and it is this class of competition that is most
provocative of the now active demand for more
aggressive anti-Indian legislation.

The tradition thus reinforced on the Natal
flank among the English people that it was impossible for a white man to do manual work
(though some German farmer-settlers ignored
and disproved it), caused diamond and gold
mining and all the complex of industries which
developed in connection with them to be based,
as farming and the Natal sugar industry had been,
on the employment of low paid non-European
labourers. When Kimberley had been made
safe for plutocracy by the fraudulent excision
of Griqualand West out of the Orange River
territory, the foundations were laid for the most
ironical tragi-comedy of capitalist Imperialism—
the exploits of the British South Africa Company
and its agents. The value of diamonds is entirely
emblematic, they are a monopolised symbol, the
blazon of solid lucre and funded property, worn
by women as an advertisement that they are
maintained by rich men, and by men as an advertisement that they are the sort that can get rich
quick and can lend you money. The special
type of instinct which Providence had implanted

in Mr Cecil Rhodes unerringly inspired him to discern that a monopoly of the supply of the finest diamonds was the most auspicious and appropriate foundation imaginable for a policy of commercial Imperialism. Recognising diamonds as a power, he associated himself with colleagues of that Oriental temperament with which they are even a passion, whether for the enhancement of personal beauty or for the inspiration of financial esteem. He succeeded by irrepressible energy, cajolery, perseverance, and unscrupulousness in amalgamating the principal interests in the diamond diggings, and established De Beers. De Beers produced and produces gigantic money-power by the employment on the one hand of a great number of low-paid black labourers under spells of from six to eighteen months close confinement, and a small number of highly-paid white men to drive them, on a few, little, fortified enclosures of African earth, and on the other by exploiting to the full the persistent human conviction that diamonds are—as Rhodes himself reverently spoke of them (see his biography)—things of "intrinsic value." De Beers made the British South Africa Chartered Company possible, of which I shall say more presently. But here I only note that De Beers reinforced by another block the growing monstrosity of the South African economic system.

The Transvaal gold-mining industry followed the lead of the diamond mines. It, too, was capitalised by outlanders, and the white skilled staff was at first recruited partly from the Kimberley mines, later from Europe. There was no reason, except the desire of capital to make big profits and quickly and the South African taboo against Kaffir's work, why the industry should not have been made and kept a white man's monopoly in all grades, till natives could enter it on Trade Union terms. "There is nothing" (I quote the Economic Commission's Report) "in the natural conditions to prevent white men from working as easily in these mines as they do elsewhere"—(for instance, in California). The conditions are much better than in most British coal mines. "The mines are well ventilated and unusually comfortable. The climate is unsurpassed, and the general health of the community excellent."

I need not review the history of the conflict between President Kruger and the mine-owning outlanders which led up to the Boer War, though it did not make that war inevitable. It was Lord Milner's determination to round off the Empire before it was too late that did that. Broadly speaking, Kruger shrewdly feared the subjection of the Transvaal to industrial capitalisation: his farmers did not want their Kaffir labour disturbed, and a modern wage-proletariat created for the Republic to deal with. As soon as the war was over, the mines, in the disorganisation of the native labour supply, demanded and obtained indentured Chinese labour. Had they succeeded in keeping it, there would by this time have been in the Transvaal a much more disquieting rival to the Natal Asiatic problem.

CHAPTER IV

THE Witwatersrand is the gigantic keystone of the arch of South African trouble. The doctrine of Kaffir work, the white land monopoly, and the mines superincumbent, the Economic Commissioners identify as its three principal causes. The mines have the reputation of being good employers: the best in South Africa. Their limbo of Hell is quite efficiently ordered. They and the diamond mines pay the highest wages to native labour, and take most pains to keep their workers in good condition, but they cannot be better than the fundamentals of the capitalist industrial employing system enable them to be. The gold mines do not in the aggregate show a high rate of profit on their capitalisation—a little over 6 per cent. all round—but they make this profit on a capitalisation increased to the utmost practicable dimensions, with a view to getting the largest possible yield of gold out of the Rand as quickly as possible. They can best keep going, as their witnesses explained to the Commission, on a basis of a small, high-paid white labour class—apparently about 15,000 *in the mines* and, *at a full supply*, about 200,000 natives. The following quotations from the Appendix to the Commission's Report sufficiently indicate the

31

relations between these two classes of labour: "The *average* white wage," on the Rand (in all grades of employment) " is 18s. 7d. per shift. The average coloured wage, including cost of rations and compound expenses, is 2s. 8d. per shift. In mining, the coloured man labours, while the white man, as a rule, directs. The mechanic has Kaffirs at hand to handle his materials and rougher tools. Compared with the mines in California, the average white miner of the Rand is less skilful, does less effective work, and receives nearly double the pay. The wages of machine drill men are on the Rand 25s. per shift (in California 12s. 6d.). Five Kaffirs do the work of handling and running two machine drills under the direction of one white contractor. The wages, food, and compound expenses of the five Kaffirs together amount to a little less than 15s. 5d. per shift, while the contractor receives (average) 30s. In hand-drill stoping, one white man directs twenty-five to thirty Kaffirs. The day's pay machine man receives 25s., and is a poor worker as a rule."

The maximum cash wage that may be paid to a Kaffir is 2s. 2⅘d. per shift.

The white man's wages, then, *for all employments* on the Rand, average seven times those of the black, including rations and housing, and in mining work with machines, done by Kaffirs bossed by white men, the proportion is from ten to one upwards. The proportion of the wages of skilled to unskilled labour in England in similar work averages fifteen to eleven—in the engineering trades about fourteen to ten. The high white wages, it is uncompromisingly recognised and stated, can only be paid on condition of natives alone being employed for all unskilled and semi-skilled labour, and being paid at a sweated wage.

The mining industry sets the standard of wages for all white South African skilled labour, and a ratio between white and black wages of from over ten to one down to six to one runs through the whole structure of industry. This direct dependence of the white worker's very high wages (the highest in the Old World) upon the very low wages of the native labourer is the secret of the philosophy of the industrial colour bar, extensively applied previously in practice, and recently embodied in legislation at the demand of the white South African Labour Party. That party is now firmly established as a section of the European aristocracy of South Africa —combined with the mine-owner and the farmer in exploiting the native African on the basis of an industrial economy and a theory of social relations derived direct from slavery. The Labour Party may not, perhaps, desire to exploit the native, but it is doing so, through the operation of the conditions thus begotten. Not unnaturally it prefers doing so to having its own wages reduced, which, in the evolved conditions under which alone the mining industry can be fully maintained, is practically the only alternative.

The furious exploitation of the gold mines,

over-capitalised, as I have said, regardless of the impending exhaustion of the deposits, can only be maintained by means of the importation of workers from Portuguese territory. The domestic supply would be insufficient, whatever wages were offered. And all South African native wages are resolutely kept down by the permanent element of compulsion inherent in the white land monopoly and the traditional colour bar. There are 1,522,000 Europeans in the Union, holding 280,000,000 acres of land; there are 4,712,000 natives, and the native reserves and locations are only about 20,000,000 acres. In the Transvaal 543,485 Europeans held, in 1924, 110,450 square miles, 1,544,151 natives 3,837. Moreover, Europeans have appropriated much of the best land for their own purposes, leaving to the natives much land of poor quality and without water, malarial, or in other respects unfit for human habitation. The native reserves and locations (except in Zululand) are admittedly inadequate and overcrowded. Col. Muller told the Empire Parliamentary Delegates to South Africa, on their visit to Umtata in 1924: "The Transkeian country under existing conditions cannot from its own resources support all its inhabitants. At any given moment nearly half the able-bodied men are earning the money for the support of their families in areas outside their territories." Ninety thousand, according to the census, were thus absent in 1921. And the Transkei is the most successful and hopeful experiment in a creditable native policy. But these reserves afford homes for many families and act as a partial means of maintenance to those who go out to work, and thus help to keep wages down below a full subsistence rate, even for the native.

The mine-owners cannot raise the rates for unskilled labour, or they would compete with the farmer. The mines were, when the Commission took its evidence, what is described as "short of labour"[1] by about fifteen or twenty thousand, on their present scale of working: and if they could enlarge their scale of employment they could make still more profit and even employ more white men, though they would not need to do so, except through the compulsion of the white Unions. As it is, they recruit 70,000 to 80,000 workers annually from Portuguese African territory. The flow of this supply is maintained for them by the operation of the Portuguese Government's forced labour system, the working of which has been very fully described after a visit to Portuguese African lands by Professor Ross of Wisconsin University, its effect being to make the Mozambique natives glad to go anywhere to earn a living outside of their own country. Professor Ross records that thousands of natives have in consequence of official exactions left that country for Nyasaland and Rhodesia, and states that the principal inducement to seek work on

[1] In 1925–26 there was a recovery. A recent report on the mining industry states that, *owing to drought and scarcity in the native reserves,* " *labour supply has been good.*"

the Rand ("where one is sure of good work and good pay") is the oppression of the Mozambique Coast natives at home. He adds that they are robbed of much of what they earn by the Portuguese officials on their return. The "good pay" is not more than 2s. 3d. per shift: their total cost to the employer, inclusive of rations and cost of recruiting averages about 18s. 6d. a week, and cannot be increased in the present economy of the industry except by reducing white men's wages, or diminishing the scale of production, and consequently the total of profit on the invested capital, and the revenues yielded by the mines to the Government,[1] the railways, the farmers, and other industries of the Union. Every class of the European community has thus a participating interest in the maintenance of the present economy of the mines, based on underpaid and partially forced native unskilled labour.

The *real* wages of skilled white workers on the Rand, notwithstanding the high cost of living, which the Commission state is due chiefly to high rents and other local prices, screwed up to exploit the industry, are higher than any similar real wages in Europe, and are exceeded only in a few of the cities of the United States. If the rate of gold extraction were slackened, if, for instance, one-third of the mines were shut down, so as to

[1] In the period 1915–16 to 1924–25 the Union Government has taken by way of taxation 38·13 per cent. of the profits of the gold industry. (Mr E. Nathan, M.L.A., in the House of Assembly, 30th April 1926.)

36

dispense entirely with the importation of Portuguese forced native labour, this would unemploy one-third of the white workers on present lines. The Labour Party naturally do not want that. There would remain, say, 10,000 white workers to 130,000 black. The margin of profit producible in the mines left working, which naturally would be the easier mines, would allow of a greater total share being paid to labour But as the mines are run on a basis of one white man paid at least £6 a week, to, on an average, thirteen black men costing 18s. 6d. each—say, £12, 6s. a week for the thirteen (£18, 6s. for the combination)—it would obviously not be possible to absorb 5000 white men dispensed with, even if 5000 more natives were discharged to make room for them, for the unit combination of fourteen, which previously cost £18, 6s., would then cost £20, 11s. 3d.—an increase of 12½ per cent. in the wages bill, which is more than all of the businesses left could afford. There would not be increased efficiency, because the present proportion of white to black is more economical than the combination would be if the proportion of whites were increased, for the natives work the drills and other machinery quite efficiently under white supervision, and could work them without. It would, in fact, be more economical for the mines to reduce the proportion of whites, as the managers are continually wanting to do. Nor, if the white labour side is left out of account, and the thirteen black men had their wages raised by an amount which

37

would cost the same—(£2, 5s. 3d.) say 3s. 6d. a week each—would that bring up the wages of unskilled labour to a civilised subsistence level even for natives who have families to support, to say nothing of white men: and the Poor Whites and all other white unskilled labourers would be left in the same position as they are to-day—unable to earn a living at current wages.

Just, therefore, as plantation slavery introduced by seventeenth century capitalist enterprise destroyed the possibility of a basis for a white industrial society, and as indentured Indian immigration contributed to that result in Natal, so there has now been forced into South Africa this huge intractable block of mining capital which can only carry on its operations with sweated native labour, has enhanced the cost of living for everyone, has made it more difficult than ever for the white wage-worker to live except at the cost of the black, and has widened still further the gap between the wage-rates of skilled and unskilled labour and the corresponding caste barrier between European and native.

The Rand Mines are a wasting asset. They will be worked out within thirty years and be failing much sooner. New gold reefs are reported in the Zoutpansberg Bushveld, but what their future may be is problematical. Platinum discoveries are causing excitement. The Government, the railways, agricultural producers and a great complex of other industries have become dependent on the mines for revenue and markets.

All these subsidiary industries have been developed conformably to the South African system of wage proportions as between white and black and to the slavery-time tradition that all manual labour is Kaffir work. And General Hertzog seeks to improve matters by enacting a colour bar against the black man; explicitly repudiating the guarantee of equal treatment which the British Crown has always professed to give him.

"When dealing with the Government of England in passing the Act of Union, the people of South Africa gave their emphatic pledges in regard to the natives who were placed in their care. They satisfied the Government of England that their natives would be dealt with with a most scrupulous justice and with the uttermost toleration. One of the greatest tasks imposed upon the white men of South Africa was to civilise and bring the natives up, and not to trample on them and repress them" (The Rt. Hon. J. X. Merriman).

CHAPTER V

THE APPLE OF DISCORD

So long as the staple industry of South Africa was pastoral and agricultural, and technical needs were sufficiently ministered to by the white and coloured skilled tradesmen, none of these had any reason for fear or jealousy of the uneducated black man as a competitor, and they did not feel any. He was just their casual labourer as he was for the farmer. He walked in the street amicably alongside the lamplighter who walked on the pavement, and turned on and lit the gas for him. He painted the tops of the lamp-posts at 2s. a day while his white boss painted the bottoms at 20s., because he could not demean himself by climbing a ladder.[1] The relations between the farmer and his Kaffirs were not intolerable. The Boers were severe masters, but not generally cruel-minded. They never treated the natives who worked for them so vilely as do the Portuguese. Their spirit was patriarchal, not commercial, and suited the native temperament the better. The Kaffir remained as a squatter on the land the white man had appropriated as his own, or came and went for such terms of service as suited him, on the farm, in the town,

[1] This example is vouched for by Maurice Evans, *Black and White in S.E. Africa.*

in the household. The domestic economy of the community, with full-grown Bantu men doing every kind of indoor service—even domestic—making the beds, wheeling the baby—is fantastic, but not oppressive: the wages are low, the work is inefficient, the whole business is incredibly wasteful and slipshod: but it has made life easy and pleasant for the white-employing and skilled artisan community: The pleasantest conditions of life, says Maurice Evans, for whites in the world. The artisan was a free worker; the relations of white boss and black labourer even in the more important trades, such as building, were not acrimonious or difficult; and this slovenly but not unworkable state of affairs might have lasted a long time without breeding much trouble had the natives been left enough land for their own tribal and domestic requirements. But the large-scale industry of the mines introduced new conditions. Manufacturing industry, had it developed extensively, might have produced like results on a smaller scale, but mining has dominated all other industrial capitalisations, and manufacturing development has been stunted. The mining industry, based on the sweating system which I have explained, could not fail to tend to break down the South African tradition of the barrier between white man's and Kaffir's work. For the black man was quite capable of doing many jobs that the white man was at first paid for, and how could the management of a capitalist industrial concern be expected to ignore

41

that fact? Inevitably the mine-managers began to try to use the black man to do the things he could do, and at the same time to go on paying him Kaffir wages. So far as there is any substantial basis for the Natal outcry against Indian competition in industries, the radical cause is similar. Capitalist industrialisation was the principal agent in converting the black man from a common convenience into a possible competitor of the white; whereas in the old, characteristic South African economy he was only his humble servant and helper, and, whether he was fairly dealt with or not, he did not compete. He was simply kept in his place. The mine exploiter could not avoid endeavouring to take him out of that place. The only class of white man by whom the Kaffir might have been felt as a competitor before industrial wage employment developed, was the Poor White; and he did not recognise him as such, as he had no notion whatever of himself doing that kind of work. It was untouchable at any price. He preferred to degenerate unemployed. The philosophy of the political alliance between the South African Labour Party and the Nationalist Party is thus simple enough. The imported European mine worker found himself in a community whose traditional first principle was and is that the white man is an aristocrat, admitting the black to no equality in Church or State, and doing no manual labour; that the black is an inferior species of animal and must be kept so. He taught the black to stope, to work machine drills and sharpen tools, and all the jobs of the mine, and took contracts for work which the black man did under his direction—at Kaffir wages. He too, as Mr Cousins says of the early settlers, "departed from the traditions" he had been raised on in Europe. The mine-manager, however, does not see white men and black men, he sees only grades of labour—and it is the technique of his training, from which he could not depart, to try to reduce his labour costs by the most economical blending of dear grades and cheap. He had the impiety to attempt to take the Kaffir out of his traditional South African place and to use him to blackleg the white man. Why not? He is not a sociologist or a politician, he is a capitalist organiser of industry. South African racial tradition and Trade Union principle, therefore, inevitably coalesce in demanding that the Kaffir shall not be given such opportunity to improve his status: a conventional colour bar is established by collective bargaining in the mines, and it is demanded that it shall be made stable by the sanction of law. The Government is also pressed by the white electorate, which alone has the vote, to apply it as far as possible in all the Public Services. No more black or coloured postmen! The cost of all public work so staffed is of course very much increased, but that is the electors' affair. The demand for a legal colour bar by the South African Labour Party appears to most persons of European civilisation outrageous, and to critical economists and sociologists insanely shortsighted. The Economic Commission flatly condemns the policy, as all previous commissions on labour questions have also done. Unionise, they say, the skilled native and fix minimum wages under the Wages Regulation Law. But excuses and explanations for the colour bar demand are easy to formulate. The white skilled miner can say: "We are not making the native's position worse than South African social convention and State policy have decreed that it should be. You assert that he cannot be made a citizen, you enforce his obedience to his employer by legal sanctions, you keep him off the pavements and tramcars, you forbid him to be abroad without a pass, you send him to bed at 9 o'clock, you—South African Europeans—have prescribed for him the permanent status of an underpaid, unskilled, servile labourer. We did not introduce this mining industry, and the South African native community might be in a much healthier state if it had never been set up. We don't mind how high you pay the native for the unskilled manual work you assign as his prerogative, but we observe that you do in fact take care to pay him only the wages of a sweated worker. We have made it possible for you to employ him profitably in your mines, and we are doing him no wrong if we limit the number of him you employ and import so that he shall not, in this gigantic imposthume of capitalised industry, be employed upon such skilled jobs as will enable you to grind down the imported European worker into a Poor White, as your time-honoured agricultural labour system has ground down its own white progeny." There is far from being no arguable excuse on such lines as these for the colour bar, the counter-arguments, however, the established conditions being such as they are, even on this plane appear to me stronger. The Economic Commission are quite clear that they are. On the plane of general statesmanship they are overwhelmingly so. I shall return to them presently.

CHAPTER VI

I HAVE sketched the progressive effects of industrial capitalisation in pinning the natives down in the status of beasts of burden and muscle-machines, and on that level foundation developing the white superstructure of the South African Commonwealth, from whose citizenship, except in the Cape Colony, they were excluded, and I have mentioned the co-operating agency of land monopoly. The enormous farms taken up by the early settlers absorbed a good deal of the country, but capitalist land speculators and syndicates have played a much bigger game. The Transvaal and Swaziland have been eaten up by them. The Economic Commission gives particulars of $4\frac{3}{4}$ million acres (about 7000 square miles) held by thirteen land companies in the Transvaal, of which $2\frac{1}{4}$ million acres are described as "unused," while on the remainder there are said to be 1058 Europeans and 10,473 natives "in occupation." Rather gingerly, for fear, no doubt, of imputations of "Bolshevism," they intimate that here is an economic reserve which might be handled to the advantage of the land-less Poor White people, if not also, directly or indirectly, to that of the natives.

But the most distinguished achievement in

46

European land policy was the result of the enterprise of the British South Africa Chartered Company, which, having obtained the patronage of the British Government on the pretext of having got a concession from the Matabele chief Lobengula to search for minerals in Mashonaland, destroyed that chief's power and proceeded to appropriate as its own the whole of the land of what is now called Southern Rhodesia. I am dealing in this Anatomy with methods of economic exploitation and their reactions on racial relations, and it is not my purpose to moralise on the astonishing history of the invasion of Matabeleland and Mashonaland, except in so far as it illustrates the essential characteristics of those methods. I have only to record what was done and its results to native land-rights. There was nothing that was admirable in the Matabele dominion, the last of the bloody tyrannies begotten by Tchaka. There was nothing that was not discreditable in the fraud, provocation, and slaughter by which its destruction was engineered. Throughout the last acts of that conflict Lobengula made a far better showing for the credit of human character than did the assailants of his domain. But Mr Rhodes was no self-seeker. He desired wealth for Imperial purposes. His one historic personal extravagance turned out most discouragingly. He aimed at getting Africa from the Cape to Cairo under the British flag. To the character of the methods by which his agents might help to accomplish this purpose, provided

that they were effectual, he was grandiosely indifferent. Originally he would have liked the
British Government straightforwardly to annex
what he wanted, but they would not do that.
Some genius in the art of facing-both-ways revived the specious Elizabethan idea of granting
a charter to a joint stock company, with authority
to exercise the administrative rights and powers
of the Crown (whatever they might be, which
was left undefined) in Mashonaland. Clive's warning and Burke's philippic against such methods,
on the text of the East India Company's rule,
were forgotten. Rhodes accepted the best he
could get. The romantic imagination of the
British public was enkindled by appropriate
journalism. Mr F. C. Selous, the renowned
destroyer of African fauna, was engaged at a large
fee to write up the auriferous promise of "Ophir."
Philanthropy and missionary zeal were enlisted.
Khama, the Bamangwato chief (whose kindred
had some old scores against Lobengula's family),
offered two thousand warriors "to help to carry
the blessings of Christianity" among the down-
trodden Mashonas. Rhodes had to be content to
rely on the combination of British idealism with
Afrikander practice. The diamond-wearing class
waxed enthusiastic, and provided directors. Dr
Jameson, after Sir H. Loch had, in the Queen's
name, repeatedly assured Lobengula, as the
Company had the British Government, that there
was no design on his land, made secret agreements
(disclosed before the Privy Council in 1916) with

a sufficient number of gentlemen-adventurers up-to-date (among them Mr Robert Coryndon, who subsequently was appointed to govern Kenya) to "smash the Matabele" in consideration of receiving each 6000 acres of land at their choice, and a share of the "loot"—*i.e.* the cattle. This agreement, of course, was made long before the factitious quarrel was picked at Victoria, which gave the excuse for the "First Matabele War" and at a date when relations with Lobengula were entirely friendly, and no ground for threatening to attack him existed.[1] After the raid, the Company usurped the ownership of the whole of the land, appropriated all the cattle they could lay hold of, and imposed forced labour, for public and private purposes, on the natives. These proceedings provoked a rebellion—suppressed by the "Second Matabele War"—after which the British Government, which had acquiesced after some faint remonstrances in the earlier proceedings, began to sit up and take a little notice.

It is important to realise and appreciate the facts with regard to native rights in lands in Rhodesia. They may well appear to English readers hardly credible. The Mashonas, who numerically predominate, had been long settled in the country when the Matabele overran them, harried and destroyed many kraals, and themselves

---

[1] But Rhodes, in 1890, when journeying in the Zoutpansberg, had assured his host, an old Boer farmer, that he intended to "end the Matabele's game and grant farms to those who assist me."

set up kraals and homesteads in parts of the country. The Southern Rhodesia Land Commission of 1925, with an African judge as its chairman, records that prior to European settlement the land was occupied by the natives (both Mashona and Matabele) according to their tribal customs and traditions. All land in a tribal area was vested in the chief, and allotments were made by him or on his behalf by sectional headmen. Each member of a family had his (or her) garden land, with certain recognised claims to fallow land; grazing was communal. The Commissioners emphasise the features of this system, of all the aspects of which their knowledge is exhaustive and unquestionable, and they conclude that "as regards agriculture the rights enjoyed by the natives, though of a somewhat precarious nature, in many respects resembled our conception of individual rather than communal tenure. As regards pasturage the tenure was more of a communal nature, but, taken as a whole, the system in its broad outlines bears a close resemblance to that obtaining in feudal times in Europe, where the copyholder had his holding of agricultural land and enjoyed rights of commonage over parts of his lord's demesne."

The charter, granted in the name of Queen Victoria to the British South Africa Company, stipulated that "careful regard shall always be had to the *customs and laws* of the class or tribe or nation, especially with respect to the *holding, possession, transfer, and disposition of lands*, and succession thereto." The Company from the outset entirely ignored this injunction and claimed and exercised unqualified ownership in fee simple of all the land in the country. The Colonial Office [1] looked on, hypnotised by the aura of the impeccable personages whose figures decked the Company's office-window, and in the Order in Council of 1898, which was issued after the Matabele Rebellion, ignored all existing rights, and vaguely prescribed that "the Company shall from time to time *assign* to the natives inhabiting Southern Rhodesia *land sufficient for their occupation*, whether as tribes or portions of tribes, and suitable for their agricultural and pastoral requirements." This was, in practice, interpreted solely as a direction to establish Native Reserves into which the natives were to be penned, thus laying the foundation of the principle of segregation. The assignment of such reserves was not completed till 1920, twenty-seven years after the invasion of Matabeleland.

What, meanwhile, was the position of the natives in their own country, the land of which was claimed and disposed of by the Chartered Company as its own? The Privy Council, in 1918, giving judgment in an action brought

[1] That Office, indeed, had no more control over the Chartered Company than the League of Nations has now over a mandated Power (the relations are closely parallel), and had far too much delicacy to act in any manner that might have been rebuffed as "inquisitorial." Short of revoking the charter, it could do nothing.

by the Crown to determine the legal position as to the land-rights claimed by the Company, declared that the land did not belong to the Company, but also that it did not belong to the natives, having been lost to the Crown through conquest, just as the land of England became nominally the property of William the Conqueror. But the Privy Council admitted that equitable rights might be conceivably proved on the basis of native law and custom, just as equitable rights were admitted and conceded in Saxon manors whose lords acknowledged fealty to the Conqueror, as the native chiefs did to the Queen. The Land Commission expressly asserts that such customary rights exist, and there can be little doubt that had they ever been argued in a British Court an equitable title in the natives to hold the lands that they thus possessed must have been admitted. They have been consistently treated as having no rights at all, but as trespassers who might be allowed to remain as tenants at will on payment of rent. Their position can hardly be more concisely and clearly expressed than it is in the Report of the Native Affairs Committee of 1910-11. "We" (*i.e.* the Company's committee-men) "see no objection to *allowing* natives to *occupy* the unalienated land of the Company (*sic*) and pay rent" (the rents demanded were 10s. to 40s. per man and 10s. for each man's wife in excess of one). "*The occupation is merely a passing phase*, the land is being rapidly acquired by settlers, *with whom the*

natives must enter into fresh agreements or leave.
We consider, too, that it would be a very short-
sighted policy to remove these natives to Reserves,
*as their services may be of great value to European
occupants"* (of their own land!). When these
words were written some Reserves had been pro-
visionally assigned, but their boundaries were not
defined, they were inadequate and natives were
liable to be removed from them if the boundaries
when settled should finally leave them outside
the Reserves. This the final fixing of boundaries
did in fact do to a good many, who were required to move their kraals. There were in 1921,
after the Reserves had been settled, 264,680
natives still living as tenants at will, subject to
rent, on lands outside the Reserves, most of
which were equitably their own property. According to the Land Commission's figures there
are now 274,372 natives so living. Such occupants are described in South African parlance as
"squatters."

The Land Commission, recently reporting,
proposed that outside the Reserves additional
areas amounting to about 7,000,000 acres should
be reserved, within which natives may purchase
land for individual ownership. They recommend
that purchase for communal tenure within these
areas shall not be permitted. They do not
recommend any gratuitous recognition of the
equitable ownership of natives, either communal
or individual, in the lands which they are now
occupying within these areas. Far less do they

53

recommend any such recognition in the area of 17,500,000 acres which they propose to allot for purchase by Europeans exclusively. On these lands they recommend that the system of allowing natives to reside upon payment of rent should, in general, be no longer permitted. But they observed that it would be unwise to abolish existing locations forthwith without due consideration of the consequences and without provision being made for those who would be moved; and they admit that in some districts it would be unfair to require them to be moved on short notice from their old homes. As farms become more intensively developed *"they will, in any case, gradually have to go,"* i.e. the buyers will turn them off; but in the meanwhile, so long as the farmer is willing to allow them to stay, those who are already paying rent should be permitted to remain during their lives. As to the natives on unalienated lands in areas to be reserved for sale to Europeans, they think the natives should be allowed to remain on these on payment of rent until the land is alienated, but that no fresh permits should be given. The Commissioners thus still withhold recognition from those equitable rights of natives in the lands they occupy which they have themselves by implication admitted must be acknowledged, and the principle of their recommendations, if pressed into execution, would ultimately mean that all natives who could not acquire freeholds in native purchase areas, should be removed into the Reserves.

The British South Africa Company had a substantial and straightforward reason for ignoring any kind of native rights in the lands whose ownership they had usurped. They were an encumbrance which depreciated the value of that land as an asset saleable in freehold to European farmers. If the Rhodesian Government, which has inherited the rights of the Chartered Company, will recognise the duty of making operative the original stipulation of the charter that native land-rights should be honoured, they will adopt the position that the rights described by the Commissioners must be admitted to a substantial validity. Where such tenure has been enjoyed by kraals, on unalienated land, whether in the area now proposed to be reserved for native purchase or in that proposed for European purchase, and also upon the alienated lands where such locations as Commissioners speak of have acquired the rights they recognise, all such occupancy ought to be respected or compensated. In the native purchase areas, even if additional communal purchase should be barred, the communal occupants already existing ought to be allowed to remain. Where such occupancies are in the European purchase area they ought to be transferred to equivalent locations either in the native purchase area or the native Reserves. Where they exist on alienated lands they ought to be transferred, with necessary compensation or assistance to migration similar to that proposed to be given to Europeans who have purchased land in areas henceforward to be reserved for natives and whom it will be necessary to transfer to unalienated lands in the European purchase areas. What justification can there be for treating Europeans more favourably in this respect than the natives?

The Commissioners say, "The majority of the natives at present understand only the communal form of tenure. . . . The natives would prefer that land in native purchase areas should be available for purchase by tribes or sections of tribes as tribal lands on communal tenure. Some have definitely asked for this provision, and where reserves are congested it is the natural and easily understandable desire. There is at least one instance of a chief and his people having purchased land in this manner." (Note the admission that some Reserves are already congested.) It appears remarkable after this preamble that the Commissioners in the next paragraph say, "*We are clearly of opinion that this form of tenure should not be permitted in the native purchase areas. We consider that the needs of the tribal natives are sufficiently met by the provisions of reserves in the Colony.*" Some of which "are congested"! It is disputed by friends of the natives that the reserves are everywhere sufficient. If communal tenure is only to be allowed in the reserves some extension of those reserves is equitably demanded.

I have written thus lengthily on this episode of the British South Africa Company's exploits and their outcome, because of their outstanding and comprehensive significance as an illustration of the combined effects of the British capitalist method for the exploitation of Africa associated with the South African tradition, generated and established as has been explained, of the rights of African natives in their relations with Europeans. Moreover, the affair was of far-reaching importance because it entrapped British authority, quite contrary to its initial intentions and contrary to its established and honourable African policy, into the new departure of treating the soil of African lands as its own and alienating it to Europeans without regard to natives' rights. That was part of the irony of the Charter episode. A further part was the resulting first introduction, under British "protection," of the policy of forced native labour, also entirely contrary to established British African policy. This was checked in Rhodesia, after the Matabele Rebellion, but the idea had taken root, and found a promising soil farther north in Kenya, where the itch for it is still very active. The Government which granted the charter, and such Imperialist enthusiasts as applauded it (who, to do them justice, would mostly have preferred direct annexation—in which case the Colonial Office could and probably would have protected the natives' rights), resolutely closed their eyes to the probable consequences of entrusting the administration of the government of an entirely helpless people, regarded habitually by the South African Europeans employed to do the rough work of subduing them as potential workers for white men, to a capitalist company, which had not only to make money for its shareholders but to bear the cost of government out of the proceeds, as far as possible, of native labour and native taxation, and by the sale of the lands on which the natives were living to European colonists. For "Ophir" had not panned out according to expectations. Mashonaland had not proved to be valuably mineralised, and the mining concession promised but scanty profits. The plan of exploitation therefore, on the ostensible basis of which the Company had been floated and chartered, had to be changed, and the development of Rhodesia as a white man's agricultural country pushed on rapidly and energetically. These consequences were quite clearly foreseen by qualified advisers of the British Government at the time, but that Government was satisfied to believe that the appointment on the directorate and as administrators of men of distinguished names and high character would suffice to ensure compliance with the intention, if not with the terms, of the charter, and the pursuit of a local policy agreeable to the standards of British public opinion. It did not, and could not, avail to do so; and the men who had to do the work on the spot, from Dr Jameson downwards, never imagined it could or intended that it should be done on those principles. Southern Rhodesia has now emerged from the position of a fief of the Chartered Company. The Government owns the unalienated lands, which are still of immense extent, and its temper and proceedings give promise of a determination that the country shall be developed with due regard to the surviving rights and liberties of natives. There is still a good deal to be done in recognition of those rights, but there is time and space to do it, and to arrest, at any rate north of the Union boundary, the further spread of the canker that threatens South Africa's future.

CHAPTER VII

CAPITALIST IMPERIALISM

THE new policy of "development" through the
agency of capitalist land companies under British
"protection" was extended under the Foreign
Office during the scramble of the "partition" in
East Africa, where "Protectorates" having been
declared, concessions of 500 and 600 square miles
were granted, and other huge estates allowed
to be set up at nominal prices, deliberately ex-
propriating the Masai from their best-watered
lands, guaranteed to them by treaty "so long
as the Masai race shall exist." The treaty
was broken, no doubt, in the interests of their
higher civilisation; the ostensible vehicle of progress, in the rear of the powder cart, being in
this case European ranching, the best land for
which purpose was in their occupation. The
Masai, not understanding the philosophy of the
Control of the Tropics, imagined that the white
man had broken faith and appropriated this land
for his personal profit. Nyasaland had already
been largely eaten up by so-called "concessions"
obtained by companies from ignorant native
chiefs; which concessions were ratified by the
British Government. More than half of the
habitable land in Swaziland was appropriated,
and all manner of monopoly privileges had been

obtained by Europeans and by the Government of the South African Republic, by "concessions" from the drunkard King Umbandine, who in native law had no power at all to make them, but which also were ratified by British authority after the Boer War. Finally, what the land speculators had spared, the British Government annexed, declaring all the lands not alienated to Europeans to be the property of the Crown, and proceeded to administer them, in practice primarily for the purposes of encouraging white settlement, with no nonsense in those early days about "sacred trusts for native inhabitants," although in theory and in name the areas dealt with were "Protectorates," and the policy of making native Reserves was enjoined.

The appropriation of the ownership of African land under this policy of capitalist development, of a character unprecedented in the history of mankind, is a very singular phenomenon. It has had some results which, to persons accustomed to take it for granted that British colonisation is governed by the principles of our own Constitution and of missionary Christianity, can hardly be made intelligible, or indeed credible, except through an understanding of its internal and spiritual history in the light of what I have written about labour and native questions in South Africa. To most home-dwelling English men and women what has happened appears unbelievable, and those who fully and truly relate the facts to them are reproved as enemies and

slanderers of their own countrymen. The ideal-
ised aspect of that method of Imperial expansion,
as presented at the time to the British public,
has been brilliantly analysed by Mr L. S. Woolf in
his *Empire and Commerce in Africa.* It was
complacently theorised for the conscience of the
philanthropic by Mr Benjamin Kidd in his book,
The Control of the Tropics. It was understood to
combine the extension of guarantees of freedom,
peace, civilisation, education, and prosperity for
the native, with those of commercial emolument
and white man's country colonisation for England. Note that it did not develop anywhere else.
West Africa and Nigeria have escaped it. They
were not "white men's country" and the
principles of British colonisation established there
were not held to be applicable. During the period
of its elaboration in South East Africa, an obscure
conflict was waged between those older traditions
of the Colonial Office and the accordant policy
advocated by Sir H. B. Loch, High Commissioner
for South Africa, on the one side, and the British
Imperialist politicians and financiers and expan-
sionist Afrikanders, abetted by the British Governments of the period and by the Foreign Office
on the other. The capitalist-commercialists
and the Afrikander policy won. Sir H. Loch
had wished to settle the problem of the un-
ruliness of the Matabele by annexation and
proper policing—and that is what, for the credit
of England, he ought to have been empowered
to do. Native land-rights would then have been

guaranteed, as they have been in West Africa. The British Government of the day was afraid to undertake that responsibility, or to risk any expenditure in thus extending the Empire. They were confident that their spoon was long enough to enable them to sup with the Devil. In consequence, as a first taste of his porridge, they got the Jameson Raid; for the purpose of which, encouraged by their proved gullibility, Mr Rhodes had jockeyed them into giving him a "jumping-off place." They got the effects of that raid on the Boer temper, and Lord Milner's determination to make a clean job of the mess. As the flood of capitalist land appropriation spread north-wards, finally reaching its limit in Kenya, it carried with it, as the earliest settlers, Boer and Afrikander farmers, who understood the traditional business of South African colonisation in such new territories. They were invited to start the colony by Sir Charles Eliot. Later, British soldiers and " public school settlers" have been introduced into Kenya, who had, when they went out, and have, no doubt, largely maintained, more characteristically English sentiments about native rights; just as in Rhodesia there quickly developed among the immigrant colonists antagonism against and disgust with the British South Africa Company and the early policy of its agents. Correspondingly, in Kenya, whereas the British public was led to believe that here was a white man's country where fine-spirited young Englishmen could settle and develop British liberty and civilisation in beneficial co-operation with natives, the early policy of the Colony was started on ultra-Afrikander capitalist lines—native land-rights overridden and ignored, large speculative land grants acquired, and pressure put by the Government on the native to force him to work for the white man. Here also the investing capitalist and landowning idea and the Afrikander slave-state mentality have been and still are in conflict with the ideas of the traditions of British colonisation. The attitude of the Kenya Die-hards towards the natives and the Indian population is a direct lineal derivative of the attitude of Afrikander theory in South Africa; and its active emergence in Kenya is the remote but recognisable outcome of the slave-policy forced by the Dutch East India Company on the first Cape Colonists.

In Kenya there are some three or four hundred English and Dutch farmers from South Africa who employ native labourers on characteristic South African lines. There are plantations of coffee, cotton, maize, sisal, and similar factory crops, intensively cultivated and dependent on the employment of large numbers of low-paid labourers. Much more land has already been taken up for such plantations than there is any possibility of working with the labour supply available; and there are large ranches for sheep or cattle, employing a few white managers and stockmen, and native shepherds and herdsmen. If white men in Kenya, instead of doing their own work, or employing white workers at white man's pay, persist in developing a planting or farming economy similar to that of South Africa, based on low-paid native labour, and do not acquire the habit of doing work themselves or employing white men at white men's wages, they will infallibly, in a generation or two, be producing a Poor White class, as in South Africa, for whom there will be no employment, and any industrial development will be producing, as in South Africa, an increasing conflict between the white and the native. Mr Atherstone, Director of Lands in Southern Rhodesia, in a special memorandum added by him to the Report of the recent Land Commission, addresses to all concerned this warning, which goes absolutely to the root of the problems of white colonisation in South and East Africa: "If the European wishes to consolidate his position in South Africa, within his own areas, he should, to an ever-increasing degree, endeavour to do more and more of his own labour."

I myself am far from thinking that the majority of the natives in those parts of Africa of which I have spoken are altogether worse off than they probably would have been by this time had British power and colonisation never intervened there— or necessarily need be in the future. But we are entering a very critical period, and if white man's policy in Africa is to continue to deal with that continent in its own economic interests, believing that those interests are necessarily and auto-

5

matically also those of the native, that policy has got to be guided with a good deal more perspicacity and enlightenment than it has shown within the boundaries of the British Empire during the last thirty or forty years—the hey-day of capitalist Imperialism.

South Africa has recently taken alarm at Mr Cousins' Report on the last South African census, in which he forecasts the increasing predominance in numbers of the black over the white population. South Africa, having a bad conscience about its dealings with natives, is afraid of the results of that preponderance, and General Hertzog has framed a policy to deal with the dangers anticipated. "Segregation" of the races is called for. Englishmen are not afraid of the preponderance of black and coloured people in the West Indies as a menace to white civilisation, because they have not a bad conscience there in regard to their dealings with them, nor in West Africa, and have no misgivings as to the capacity of what is essential and valuable in what they think of as Western civilisation to maintain its leadership. The Western civilised man, if he sticks to the ethical principles which have made Western civilisation, will always lead in such communities, whether he be white, coloured, or black, unless he destroys his forces by parasitism and creates an irreconcilable Jacquerie of oppressed and dissatisfied natives capable of undermining, corrupting and swamping him. Such a fate can more easily overtake a white aristocratic community, de-

66

pendent entirely, as white South Africa is in all its economic functions, on such a servile labouring population, than it is likely to overtake organised capitalism in Europe through any evolution of the power of the wage-earning classes.

CHAPTER VIII

SEGREGATION

"SEGREGATION"—"the policy of Segregation"—
what does it mean? It might mean what Sir
Theophilus Shepstone's native policy meant in
Natal: that the European colonists should leave
the native peoples sufficient land, in their own
tenure of tribal communal ownership, and allow
their communities to develop according to their
peculiar genius. The characteristic Bantu community was a fundamentally communist-socialist
corporation with a very stringent system of social
law and custom, not formally democratic, but
dominated by social need, enforced by the
sanctioned authority of the father over his children
(no matter what their age), of the headman over
the householder, of the tribal chief over the
headman, the paramount over the tribal chief.
Whatever a man does, he is responsible to the
tribe, for he is part of its tissue. What he earns
belongs to the family or the tribe, represented by
the father and the chief; what he has to pay, his
chief or his father pays for him.

The chief's official power (before white men
tampered with it) was a "dictatorship of the
proletariat," exercised through a Tcheka of witch-
doctors, through smelling out, the civic duty of
delation (informing against any transgressor of the

principles of communal health enforced by the unseen world) and the prompt killing or "eating up" of offenders or suspects (as in David's dealing with Achan. In the case of Bathsheba, David was himself smelt out by the witch-doctor Nathan, who "put his mouth" on the baby so that it died). Lobengula's methods of political discipline—murder and cudgelling—and his style of diplomatic and parliamentary oratory strikingly anticipated those of Signor Mussolini, whose public aims are intrinsically the same—the protection and aggrandisement of his own people. He hectored Mr Rochfort Macguire, squatted upon the cow-dung at Bulawayo, as Mr Tomski would address Mr J. H. Thomas grovelling in the Parliamentary Labour Party. He was a tyrant— a great African chief had to be. He practised the merciless traditions of his own dynasty. But he was a very able and tribal-spirited man. British rule deposes the paramount chief, and substitutes the Crown. The Chartered Company pulled the lynch-pin out of the Matabele tribal system by excluding Lobengula's descendants from any authority. The white man's magistrate supersedes the chief's judicial powers: revenue officers encroach on his finance. But the dissolution of native tribalism which is inevitably induced by contact with white civilisation goes much further and deeper than that. It individualises the native, soul and body. It taxes him as an individual. He is made to pay his own hut tax and consequently repudiates his father's control. He draws his own wages and ceases to account for them to his chief. As a squatter or labour tenant on the land that the white man has occupied, he attorns to him as a landlord. His duty of obedience is by law transferred to him. Law he respects. The white man, under his Masters and Servants Law, commands his labour: the chief ceases to do so. He breeds and speculates in cattle on his own private account. He gets education, adapts himself to the industrial life of the town, and in a hundred ways becomes more and more dissociated from the matrix of tribal motive, custom and duty, and more and more indoctrinated, subjected, exercised and made dependent by the influences and necessities of his European occupation, civilisation, economic position and, sometimes, religion. In thousands he loses all intimate connection with tribalism; his children grow up undisciplined by it. If he does not thus lose contact with his tribe, but goes back to its location periodically, this interchange is constantly reacting upon its own internal history. It is impossible that tribal civilisation, even with the fullest possible organisation of native self-government, should now under any system of segregation develop on its own "natural" lines. Its evolution must inevitably be profoundly affected by European supremacy, contact, and intercourse.

No white politician and no educated native in Africa really thinks of a true segregation when he employs that word. The most that those

who mean the very most by it contemplate is that
natives shall have their homes in blocks of territory fully sufficient for their economic maintenance, and to provide for their increase. They
must learn, they can learn, but they can only
learn from Europeans, how to make their agriculture and stock-handling much more productive
than it is under their traditional methods: they
must learn, can learn, but can only learn from
Europeans how to develop their economic resources by other arts and industries. Unless
this is done, no extent of reserves will long suffice
them, and over-population and overstocking with
cattle will be breeding trouble again. It is best
that European intervention in such territory
should be restricted (as it is in the Cape native
territories) to such helpful and educational purposes. Native finance has to be organised, by
Europeans, to meet new public expenses. Natives
will go out of their reserves to work for European
employers. Even if it could be imagined that
they need never have done so, it is quite certain
that under any practicable system of segregation
they will continue to do so now. The indis-
pensable basis of the whole economic life of
white South Africa being Kaffir work, it is
obvious that not one European in a hundred—
and no one whom the majority would not regard
as a visionary—who advocates "segregation," has
any idea of sorting out and resettling the country
in black and white substates, each economically
self-supporting. Comparatively few professing

segregationists would not regard even such a
degree of segregation as I have just sketched as
an extravagant policy far too liberal and indulgent
to the native. And, indeed, it is not more than
partially practicable. More than half the natives,
from compulsion of landlessness, live outside the
native reserves and locations, and work for white
men. Any increased provision of land for them
in pursuance of a segregation policy would no
doubt diminish, at any rate at first, the pressure
forcing Kaffirs into the labour market. But no
policy of additional provision of land and segregation can in practice be carried into effect so
rapidly and thoroughly as seriously to affect the
labour supply: even if the black population were
not increasing rapidly. But the farmers are
nervous about any real concession to the natives.
They do not want even a segregation policy that
would do as much as and no more than carry
out the ideas expressed by General Botha in
passing his Land Bill of 1913, when he said:

> "Why did the native problem remain such
> a difficult one? Simply because the native
> had got as much right to the country as the
> white man. *Some people thought the solution
> of the native problem meant the finding of
> sufficient labour for their own requirements.*
> The Government could not supply their
> labour by legislation, they might facilitate
> the obtaining of labour: that was all.
> Above all, their laws must be fair and equit-

able, of a kind which would have the effect of developing their people. If there was one thing the European must keep before him, it was the improvement and development of their people. *Let the native people keep their traditions and build up along those lines.* . . . The white man must do nothing to oppress the native. In the Union there was no room for oppression, there was only room for justice and good honest legislation."

Now examine what "segregation" means, approaching it from the other side—that of the European. White men do not want Kaffir families about their house-places, Kaffir kraals on their farms, or Kaffir locations against their boundaries. They do not want the natives' untidiness, their noises, their odours. There is much in their habits repulsive to Europeans, with which white people hate their children to become familiarised. They do not want to be plagued by their thieving: they do not want their piratical dogs, their meagre, ravenous goats, their scabby sheep, their ploughshare-headed pigs, their ungelded runts, their tick-encrusted cattle about their farms. For the sake of labour a certain measure of these nuisances has to be tolerated, but native "squatters," and still more native kraals and locations, adjacent to any white man's property diminish both its amenity and its economic value for Europeans. That is a stubborn fact, and must obviously continue to exercise, as it does, great influence on European views of agrarian and native policy.

The Natives Land Act of 1913 was conceived of as proposing to achieve a separation of natives and Europeans by marking out areas within each one of which all land should, through the machinery of the Act, eventually come to be held solely by one race, so that the map would present the aspect of a chess-board or crazy quilt of intermingled white and black areas. But natives were still to be working everywhere on the white men's farms. But anything that with any appropriate meaning could be called "segregation" is now, (1) physically and geographically impossible, having regard to the established distribution of the white and black population and the kind of lands necessary and available for their residence; and (2) from the point of view of the means of livelihood of the native population and the needs of the European farmer, unworkable. Five-ninths of the black population, in the census of 1921, were found outside of native reserves and locations, and that meant that many more than five-ninths of the adult males were earning their living outside of them. It has proved impossible to provide for the augmenting of native landholdings under the plan of allotting new exclusive native areas, proposed in Botha's Land Act of 1913, which really was intended to promote segregation. Europeans have, since that Act was passed, been allowed to buy Crown lands in those areas; and the numbers of natives to which the Census

Commissioners' statement applies must have largely increased during the five years since 1921.

If the native had enough land to live on, with adequate water-supply or storage, and had learnt to make economical use of that land by improved agriculture, it might conceivably be possible for large blocks of the native community to become self-supporting. But, even looking only at the natives' side of the question, the development of an entirely self-supporting native peasantry would take many years to accomplish. Looked at from the white man's side, the process would mean the withdrawal of much of the labour by which, as we have seen, the dominant European, who does not do his own work, lives, and the mere beginning of it would cripple the operations of many farmers. An increasing flood of Poor Whites would be generated, who would have to change their habits and work. If land could be found for these—and it is difficult enough to find land for all those of them who need it at present—they would have to set to and work it without Kaffir labour. It would indeed be a good thing if they were to do so, but they are unlikely to change habits suddenly. If other white farmers employed them, they would have to pay them at least three or four times as much as they now pay the native, or the degradation of the landless white would accelerate. So the farmers do not want real segregation. What they want is quite simple and natural. They do not want native farms mixed up with theirs, or native locations

75

against their farm boundaries. They do not want "squatters" occupying part of their land or that of their neighbours, and living independently by their scratching and scrambling farming. They want labourers under the Masters and Servants Law, or they want all their black "by-woners" to be "labour tenants," also under the Masters and Servants Law. If the labourers have families, they would prefer that these should be "segregated" in some native reserve or location—the farther away the better—and that the "boys" should be working for them on a six months' or longer contract.

Now it is imaginable that the life of an African agricultural community, whether in the Union, Rhodesia, or Kenya, could be carried on with the best attainable material advantages to both parties under a system in which natives who own, or whose tribes or families own, land in native reserves come out for terms of labour on white men's farms. The contracts or laws under which they should do so may be better or worse, reasonable or objectionable; that is an administrative, not an economic, question. The Economic Commission thinks the existing Masters and Servants Laws are a safeguard to the servant, which it is advisable to retain. The South African courts of justice have a high reputation for administering these laws justly. And it may be expedient that such contract labour should be supplemented by labour-tenant or, as it is called in Kenya, "squatter" labour—the native residing with his family on the land and having the use of part of it for himself. But such a system would not segregate, and it tends to bar segregation and defeat its ideal purposes, as conceived by those who advocate it on behalf of the native; because it breaks up the economic basis of native society and hinders the development of native peasant agriculture by withdrawing the able-bodied men from their own cultivations, and breaks up its social basis, by destroying the family system and parental and tribal authority. Many people, on the other hand, may think that a desirable process. It Europeanises and educates the native. But it is not segregation. The contract labourer may return and marry. He will then (as the reserve cannot support him) either have to leave his wife at home and re-engage as a servant, or find a place as a labour tenant.

It will be seen that General Hertzog's Native Land Bill, which I shall presently examine, abandons the principle of segregation aimed at in General Botha's Land Act of 1913. It appears, therefore, time that that inappropriate and misleading term should cease to be used as descriptive of South African native land policy. Even in Southern Rhodesia, where the policy is more whole-heartedly entertained, and where a nearer approach can be made to its partial realisation, it is inaccurate. It is not proposed that white men there shall dispense with native labour; and in some districts of Southern Rhodesia, as throughout the greater part of the Union terri-

tories, native and European rights of landholding
must, perforce, be left intermixed to such a degree
as to render the use of the term "segregation"
nonsensical.

The Governor of Southern Rhodesia recently
put the facts perfectly clearly.   I quote his words:

"Absolute segregation of the natives—that
is their removal from all relationship and all
contact with the white races—would be
impracticable and disastrous. It would be
disastrous to the native population, for it
would condemn them to moral, intellectual,
and material stagnation, and experience has
shown that to keep the African races on the
path of progress the constant stimulus of
contact with European races is essential."
[*A voice:* "What about the Portuguese
race?"] "When that influence is withdrawn,
retrogression is rapid and certain. No time
must be lost if Southern Rhodesia is to learn
from the experiences of the Union, and avoid
the difficulties that now confront them in
regard to the native land question. We cannot, however, prevent the ambitious and
advanced natives from desiring to emancipate
themselves from the control of their chiefs
and from forsaking the stagnant communal
life of the kraal for a life of greater independence and opportunity. It is to the advantage, and to the advantage of the country
generally, that natives should have their

78

reserves and work under Europeans on farms and mines."

The imaginable ideal of a segregation policy, convenient to both European and native, is this: that the native and his families should live either tribally or—under the system of personal tenure (freehold or leasehold) as fostered and growing up in the Cape Native territories—as a peasant cultivator, in self-contained locations sufficiently large or sufficiently close together to enable him to develop the institutions of local self-government, which a progressive, agricultural, and social civilisation makes necessary for him, but that he and his sons shall go out of these locations at times convenient to them to labour for the European in his separate locations on his farms or in his mines, or in his households. Many natives would certainly do so. They will progressively want more money, even when they have land, than the marketable produce of their own land can earn for them. But in order to maintain the supplies of hired labour, if the native had his rights in regard to land, it would doubtless be necessary to pay him more than, as now, 15s. to 20s. per month and rations. That is the first snag at which the European farmer voter, who outnumbers all other classes, and whose consent the Government has to command, stumbles. He baulked at it badly in Kenya under the influence of Afrikander traditions, and at the outset prevailed, but his policy of land restriction

79

and forced labour has now been, at any rate for a time, defeated there, provided that the Colonial Office stands firm in maintaining the position into which it was, somewhat reluctantly, forced a few years ago by British public opinion. Mr Ormsby Gore (Under-Secretary of State for Dominions) assured Parliament lately that he was perfectly satisfied that the Kenya native people are advancing and that Kenya offers more opportunities and more scope for the study and solution of the problem of the intercourse of one civilisation with another than any other part of the world. In Kenya they were seeing the working out of the dual policy of giving *absolutely free choice* to the native as to whether he stays in the reserves or comes out and lives and associates with Europeans in agricultural work. He was as anxious as anyone "to give the natives a square deal, and, eliminating all forms of compulsory labour, to secure true progress, true education, and true development for all His Majesty's subjects, whether black or white."

That combination of interests, however, even if it is workable in South Africa, which the farmers are not yet prepared to believe it to be, does not spell segregation. The farms are immense. The distances are enormous. Farm labourers must reside, while they work, on their employers' land. They will not be contented to live as single men in barracks. South African land policy aims at getting rid of "squatters." In Kenya, on the other hand, the policy of establishing what are there termed "squatters" is being advocated, in order to secure a farm labour supply. What is contemplated there, however, is apparently what would be called in South Africa "labour tenant." Whatever name is used, what is recognised in both countries is that if the native is to be induced to work for the European he will require some land for his own use and that of his family. The Kenya agricultural system is young and its arrangements are still experimental. If a system of "squatter tenants" or "labour tenants" at will is found satisfactory there, either to white or black, it will be contrary to experience wherever else it has been tried in a mixed white and African community. The "squatter" labour tenant is likely to become in the eyes of the European a nuisance, for the same reasons that he is considered so in South Africa, and as the squatter tenant is in the West Indies by any improving landowner. The African will not improve his own cultivation under that tenure. He is not satisfied with the position of tenant. He wants to own his own land, and in the areas where he is domiciled for the purpose of working for the white man, he will be always dissatisfied if he cannot acquire land of his own. And the longer, the more completely he is separated from his tribal locations and acquires the habits of the European community among which he is working (and which it is assumed is going to affect him educationally) the more unreasonable and difficult will it become to resist this demand. Already in South Africa, as was the case in Jamaica after emancipation, white landowners and farmers prefer to sell out their farms to associations of natives to continuing either to work them with labour tenants or to rent them to "squatters." It is difficult, therefore, to imagine that the policy of so-called "European" areas, in which natives are to be employed, but not to own land, is likely to be stable. But no doubt it may work for a time.

The policy of establishing in South Africa separate property areas for Europeans and natives is, however, now favoured both by friends of the natives in their interests and in those of the European community. It must be accepted that the policy is generally considered desirable, and that the endeavour to carry it out will be pressed. It is desired to evolve, as far as possible, a piebald map, as contemplated by the 1913 Law, and in Southern Rhodesia by the recent report of the Land Commission in that colony. It will, however, certainly be necessary to have in the Union also neutral or mixed areas as recommended for some areas in Southern Rhodesia, because the complete sorting out and separation of settlement is already recognised outside the reserve to be impracticable. It is impracticable over the greatest part of the territories within the Union, where there is any considerable native population. That is why the Union Government's most recent proposals do not aim at segregation, but only at delimiting the neutral or mixed districts, leaving the established exclusive native reserves, and as many exclusive European reserves as possible, outside of these.

The policy is a temporary makeshift; but need not therefore be condemned. The Economic Commission, however, do not consider it worth attempting. Either, they say, in discussing the segregation policy, "it must be believed that it is both possible and desirable to keep the native *out of European industry* and leave him (in areas reserved exclusively for his native occupation and in which alone he may live) to develop an independent economy of his own, or it is necessary to contemplate the ultimate absorption of the native in European industry and his assimilation to European institutions." Whether the complete realisation of the latter alternative is necessary and inevitable or not (and in any case it can be delayed or accelerated by deliberate policy), the complete realisation of the former is quite impossible. For, say the Commissioners, stating the facts of the situation very moderately but in carefully chosen and quite incontrovertible sentences, "the contact of native and European has lasted too long and their economic co-operation is too intimate and well established for the native to be excluded from European areas and European industries. The provision of adequate native reserves has been delayed too long for it to be possible now to provide reserves within which it would be possible for the present native population of the Union to live without dependence on outside employment: and it was for too long the

83

policy of the Union *to drive the native by taxation and other devices to work for Europeans* for it to be possible now to exclude him from the field of employment he is occupying."

The Government of Kenya, as I have said, has recently been forced by British opinion to amend its declared earlier policy of compelling natives by law to work on white men's estates; but it still maintains the "device" of driving them by taxation to do so. This form of pressure, however, has also been somewhat relaxed, and is less frankly advocated than formerly. The recognition that the proceeds of direct taxation of natives ought at least to be applied for their benefit is also gaining ground.

CHAPTER IX

AFRIKANDERUS CONTRA MUNDUM

To anyone who appreciates and admires the qualities of European South Africans, it has been disquieting to observe in recent years an increasing emergence in acts of policy and manifestations of Afrikander opinion a temper in regard to the native population which appears to recognise no alternative to a defeatist fatalism but an abject campaign of repressionism—to block the native from industrial advance, to diminish his contact with and his interests in white civilisation, to curtail his civil rights, to keep down his earnings, and simultaneously to whimper that he competes disastrously with the white man because of his low standard of living.

If it may be assumed that the European's dealings with the natives and the relations in which he now stands to him are just, wise, and humane, or at any rate defensible, and that the European desires and intends to maintain just, wise, and humane relations with him, or if the relations are at present in any degree unjust, unwise, and oppressive, to rectify and redress them, it is not at first easy to apprehend precisely, in any form that appears even conjecturally very convincing, what are the disastrous developments that the alarmist party in South Africa

85

fear will result from the increase of the native population.

The clearest and most concise statement I have seen of the character of these fears was given by Sir Thomas Watt, M.L.A. for Dundee, Natal (formerly a Minister), in a letter to the *Times* of 30th March 1926. The letter was evoked by the controversy about Indian rights; but it covered the whole philosophy of the relations between white and coloured.

"The white man, English as well as Dutch, is determined to do all he can to remain, and what is more, to rule. He hopes to get the sympathy and support of the Mother Country. If that is withheld he will not be deterred. To those who say that England cannot be a party to a great act of injustice, I would reply that this matter is, to us in South Africa, such a vital and fundamental matter, that no ethical considerations, such as the rights of man and equal opportunities for all non-Europeans, will be allowed to stand in the way. It is a question of self-preservation with us. We are now a self-governing nation with full power to manage our own affairs. Naturally, we recognise our duties and responsibilities to those under our control, and also our position as part of the Empire.

"We do not allow the natives the vote except in the Cape Province: we do not permit them to acquire land outside certain definite areas, or to get drink, or to hold firearms, or to visit labour centres looking for work without an official pass. Europeans in South Africa have a deep, instinctive, and abiding feeling that, if they and their descendants are to remain there, they must not give full political and other rights to the blacks, who outnumber them by four to one.[1]

"They may be, as some hold they are, committing a great wrong to a people for whom they are trustees, and they may raise enmities and forces that will all the more surely and quickly destroy themselves; but they do not think so, and they must be left to manage or mismanage their own affairs."

Sir Thomas Watt does not perhaps here help us very much to realise what are the disastrous developments feared—except that if Europeans give full political and other "rights" to the blacks they may not "be able to remain and rule" in South Africa. The word "rights" is ambiguous, and may be used in two senses: (1) legal, as meaning liberties and privileges, secured or not forbidden by law, which is perfectly definite and capable of being applied by the courts, as in the Hildick-Smith colour bar case; and (2) "moral" (that term is also ambiguous, but it will serve as commonly understood) or "ethical," which is the word that Sir Thomas Watt himself uses when he says that "no ethical considerations will be allowed to stand in the way" of South African Europeans perpetrating great acts of injustice, if that is the only way to enable them to remain and, what is more, to rule. I wish that Sir

---

[1] Actually at present about three to one.—O.

Thomas Watt had shown us how the recognition of anything that he would admit to be an ethical or moral right of the native will make it impossible for Europeans to remain in South Africa or to maintain their political and social leadership, and, more importantly, why he believes that the withholding of such ethical or moral rights of the native is likely to ensure Europeans being able to remain and rule. He and those who share his position appear to be victims of some mechanical or arithmetical superstition about society, a pusillanimous disbelief in the potency of the qualities on which they themselves specially plume themselves as Europeans. There are quite a number of human virtues in which Europeans are obviously in no wise superior to the natives—for one example, courage — and it is only in respect of qualities other than these and because of such qualities that European civilisation is stronger than African. These qualities alone give Europeans any justification for supposing that they can, under any circumstances, maintain their social standards and their supremacy, even by the most thoroughgoing repressionism, among a rapidly multiplying population of hostile natives. If this defeatist mentality is well grounded (and it is part of the purpose of this Anatomy to point out in what respects it is), and if Europeans do not purge themselves of its causes, which lie largely in their own slave-state mentality, then the only method by which they can hope to remain and rule in South Africa is to achieve a true segregation, to eliminate or exterminate the natives from all the areas in which the European desires to remain, and to remain there and rule themselves, and do their own work. Which, of course, it is nonsensical to talk about. It cannot be done, and it would not be done if it could be. Europeans do not desire it.

The issues of practical statesmanship which are material in these questions are confused by referring, as does Sir Thomas Watt, to police regulations, as if they were an interference with moral or ethical rights; talking as if because it is justifiable to forbid the holding of firearms or the consumption of spirituous drinks, it is equally open to Europeans to interfere with the natives in any other manner that they may imagine to be in their own interests. To say that no ethical considerations will be allowed to stand in the way is mere superficial and random bombast. Those who talk thus could learn a lesson in clear-headedness from a "Transvaal Farmer Politician," quoted by Professor Jabavu in a recent paper on South African problems. (*Review of Missions,* July 1924.)

"General Hertzog's solution is impossible. It can only mean the extermination of the native, and such a solution the white man will strenuously oppose, not because he loves the Kaffir so much, not because he needs the Kaffir so badly, but simply because there is such a thing as right and justice, and because our deep-rooted Christian civilisation prevents our flying to remedies which are elemental, even if we had the power or strength to make use of them. Indeed, it is just this ingrained conception of fairness and equity that makes the problem so difficult. We wish to employ Christian principles, but apparently we cannot do so without committing suicide."

"We do not believe," comments Professor Jabavu, "that the application of the principles of Christianity to economics is suicidal; but the duty of proving and preaching this falls to the Church." The Dutch Reformed Church, however, formally excludes natives from participation in the benefits of its philosophy and apparently does not concern itself to apply it to them. Sir T. Watt and those who share his outlook may be assured that they certainly will not have the sympathy of the Mother Country or of any other community of civilised mankind outside South Africa in the principles of policy to whose guidance he appears to be prepared to commit himself. No intelligent statesman will share his illusion that Europeans in South Africa are likely to be able permanently to establish their hegemony upon such lines. He may retort that that is only their own affair. The European world, and still more the African and Asiatic worlds, are not likely to flatter themselves that it is so. They will not be content to acquiesce silently in this "firing of haystacks," [1] even if the riskiness of the

[1] General Smuts's description of the Anti-Indian and Colour Bar Bill.

policy were their only ground of objection. They will not be deterred from examining African problems from the point of view of the African native and of "ethical considerations." They will not be prepared, by abstaining from speaking their minds, to betray their fellow Europeans in South Africa who object to a British Dominion outspokenly adopting the principles of a Portuguese African Government.

For any guidance of statesmanship Sir Thomas Watt's defiant generalisations are quite unprofitable. The practical question for statesmanship is—what does the native need and what liberties or rights are those that he feels it an injustice that he should be denied?—and can the European say that his claims in respect of these have no moral validity? Take two mentioned in Sir Thomas Watt's list. First, the Vote. The native has it in the Cape Province, preserved to him by the South Africa Act when the Union Government was established. The right to registration as a voter may be altered by a two-thirds vote of both Houses of Parliament sitting together, but no person already on the register can—without violation of the express provision of the South Africa Act, "be removed from the register by reason only of any disqualification based only on race or colour" (General Hertzog apparently proposes to ignore this provision of the Constitution). The Cape natives do not desire to be disfranchised: they would consider it unjust that their registration should be forbidden, and illegal that those already registered should be disfranchised. No European can pretend that he would not think so too. This, then, doubtless, is one of those cases in which Sir Thomas Watt would not allow "ethical considerations" (or even legal) to stand in the way. But does the Cape native franchise threaten—has it ever threatened, or in the slightest degree practically affected European residence, rule, or leadership in the Cape Colony or the Union? Obviously not. Natives have not the vote outside of the Cape. Do they want it? Is their lack of it a disquieting grievance? Or would it be so if Native Affairs Departments were helped to be more efficient and better provided with funds? Surely not yet sufficiently so as to make it worth while to stir the franchise question at all; certainly not by disfranchisement in the Cape to take an overt step of aggression on the part of the white against the black, the complement of the Colour Bar Law in the gambit of repressionism. The effect on native feelings in the Union, on the temper of black and coloured peoples throughout the rest of Africa and the world towards the whites is bound to be affected by such overt moves in a campaign of repressionism in a degree the mischief of which will be out of all proportion to the reinforcement which such defiances of "ethical considerations" can possibly give to the power of the white in South Africa. There are some things of questionable general equity, or even of disadvantage to individuals which can be done with impunity or with apparent public advantage, and some which cannot. Withdrawal of political franchise is one of the latter. It is too symbolical, too crudely manifest an announcement of mobilisation against native rights.

CHAPTER X

THE LAND GRIEVANCE

THE first thing almost any writer on African questions will tell about the native is that what he most wants, is most anxious over, most suspects the white man's dealings with him about, is land. Why? Savage tribes in uncolonised parts of the world not familiar with the institution of landed property have shown no such solicitude about land. They have often been willing, before they learnt to know the white man's ways and when there was room for both, to allow white men to occupy. The white man cannot profitably do this except upon his own terms and those of his private landowning system. The South African native is now so excessively cumbered and suspicious about land as he is, because he knows through experience that the white man has taken away and will take away from him—calling that his private property which before was no man's property—not only such land as he immediately needs for his own support, but all the land he can possibly push him out of, except on terms of working as his servant. That is the land policy just now in the ascendant in the South African Union. The European has uses for land without using it. The individual native cannot say certain land is

94

his. The idea of private ownership of land is an absurdity it takes him long to imagine. "Very well then," says the white man, "it shall be mine."

The process of land settlement has resulted in 1,520,000 Europeans owning about 280,000,000 acres, and 4,700,000 natives retaining recognised communal rights in about 20,000,000 acres. 587,000 natives are employed in urban areas, and of the remaining 4,113,000 about half are living on white men's land outside the reserves and locations. Many of these 2,000,000 have at least as good a right to the land as the white man has. His title over much of the country originates merely in his father or grandfather having arrived and having said, "This land is mine! Snap!" and grabbing it as if he were playing a children's game. There is[1] nothing more in white man's land law among Bantu natives than that, and no one pretends that there is.

The native can get no redress for the iniquities of his position under the white man's law. He has no title. "Whoever," said Lord Sumner in his judgment on the Southern Rhodesia Lands case, "now owns the unalienated land" (*i.e.* lands not already sold by the Chartered Company to Europeans) "the natives do not. . . . The Company's alienations by grant (of all the rest of the land) are unquestionably valid: the natives have no share in them." That is the principle on which white men have acted in South

[1] Fundamentally, of course, there is nothing more in our own.

95

Africa, not indeed troubling themselves at the time about legality; but, as it turned out in Rhodesia, quite legally under British law; which it was comforting to find out was the case. Lord Ripon really had not a leg to stand upon when he protested against the granting out of the land (under Dr Jameson's secret agreement) "*contrary to the promise of the Chartered Company, and contrary to the public declarations and intentions of the Government.*" These alienations were "unquestionably valid." The Company had only exercised latent Crown powers impliedly deputed to them. The natives counted for nothing. There was plenty of room—there still is plenty of room for many years—for both native and white occupation of land in South Africa, even within the Union territories, for subsistence purposes: but no! wherever the physical resistance of native tribes could be overcome, there white men have declared and effected their fee-simple ownership, each up to his neighbour's boundaries, and permit the native to live there in his ancestral communal homes, or as a squatter or labour tenant, only on sufferance and on payment of rent in money or service.

That these facts should be acknowledged and plainly stated, instead of being burked or glossed over as they usually are by writers about the British Empire, does not create enmity in the mind of the native against the European: they are never out of the native's mind; and it would be a complacent illusion to imagine that they are, and that they do not produce their natural effect on his sentiments towards the white man, however discreetly he may dissemble them. Hence that distrust and suspicion on his part which, to devout Imperialists, often seems so deplorably misconceived.

It is in regard to land then that, in this Anatomy, those "ethical considerations" which Sir Thomas Watt has assured us South Africans are prepared to ignore, have most practical relevance. Land, unquestionably, is one of the things the native wants and cares about. The white man's ownership of fourteen-fifteenths of the land within the Union (of which, however, one must remember about half is so barren and rainless and scantily habitable that it may practically be left out of account) has not been established with any inconvenient degree of regard to ethical considerations. White men took what they wanted and all they could get, with a view to their own maintenance or enrichment. In large areas colonised by the Boers there were no resident natives or very few, and no one would pretend that the Bantu tribes that were resident in various parts of the country when the white men began to trek had any kind of right to a land monopoly as against European immigrants. They, too, were recent comers. General Botha's proposition that the native has "as much right" as the white man is quite fair enough for the natives' case. The manner in which the white man has colonised shows, however, little trace of an admission of that proposition. No equitable division was possible. If the Boer farmer was to settle and live, the native, being an unabashed cattle stealer, like the Scottish Highlander, had to be driven away to a desirable distance, or allowed to remain only under conditions in which he could be kept in order. The foundations of the present preposterous inequality between the land ownership of the natives and that of the Europeans in the Boer territories are to be recognised in the long conflict of the period of settlement. The startlingly paradoxical statement made by General Hertzog recently in the Union Parliament, that the European has to "fight an unequal fight against the native," is not, as a reflection of past experiences, intrinsically quite so absurd as it must at first appear. If the Bantu had been good neighbours and had been capable of quietly carrying on their own tribal economy where the white man found them without molesting him, there would have been much more possibility of their equitable rights to land being fairly acknowledged and settled. Europeans in the earlier days of expansion did not gratuitously raid, massacre, and steal cattle as did T'chaka's warriors. But they were determined to settle and farm, as they had every right to do, and to take all necessary means to protect themselves from interference by natives. They killed out the Bushmen, as the Bantu had done before them, because the Bushmen were untamable fighters and cattle thieves, and competed with them as hunters of game. They could not be lived alongside of without risk: and the Boers could not afford to take risks. These ethics of a militant colonisation in regard to land tenure were accepted and carried forward as axiomatic when the economic policy of capitalist land appropriation supervened on the necessities of a pastoral farming settlement, just as capitalist industrialism accepted as axiomatic the slavery-bred Afrikander theory of Kaffir work and Kaffir pay. The resulting present distribution of legally recognised ownership in some parts of South Africa is a crying iniquity which responsible statesmen of all parties admit to be so, and not only do not defend but insist must be remedied. Less valiant-mouthed than Sir Thomas Watt, they assert a need to redress it on ethical grounds—they agree that natives have a *right* to have some more land, that justice must be done to them in this matter, and that they are suffering injustice in the position in which they have been left by this process of settlement. "I want," says General Hertzog, "to see the native in possession of the land which became his heritage under the law of 1913."

Justice could be done to the native community in regard to their equitable rights to land without injustice to the European community, if any South African Government were strong enough to undertake and carry through the task. If no Government can be found strong enough to achieve it, no Government is going to be strong enough to maintain the stability of European supremacy in South Africa on the basis of the existing and increasing injustice of the present land distribution.

The white man has acquired for himself, gratuitously or at nominal prices, the ownership of by far the greater part of the country, excluding the black man—43½ acres per head for whites against 1 acre per head for the natives. The Beaumont Native Lands Commission, set up under the Natives Land Act of 1913, reported years ago that the natives then needed another 20,000,000 acres—just twice what they had. *This* amount of land, at least, ought to have been *given* back to them, set apart in trust for them in suitable areas. The European, on any basis of judgment, assuming that he will admit any rights at all for the black as against the white, has taken too much of the land in South African territories for himself and has left the native too little. If justice is to be done, if even the threat of inevitably increasing resentment is to be mitigated, the European ought to give up, without making the natives pay any monopoly price for it, at least enough land to present a decent appearance of putting the native back on something like a level position, such as in a peaceful and equitable original division of the land would have been conceded to him. This is what it is proposed to attempt to do in Southern Rhodesia. Opinions may differ as to the justice or wisdom of reserving for Europeans so much land as the Rhodesian Land Commissioners propose, but they do at least propose to allow as much land for the natives as they can now use, or are likely to want to use, for a reasonably computed period. This can still be done in Rhodesia, because there is sufficient unalienated land in the Government's hands, and because the transfer from Europeans to natives can be made in some other parts without prohibitive cost and difficulty. It cannot be done in the Union without taking back some of the land required from Europeans. But it is not only no less necessary, but in fact far more urgently necessary in the Union than in Rhodesia that such provision for the natives should be made.

The existing injustice is of a very definite and obvious kind. The white man, victoriously waging not an "unequal fight" but an admittedly dangerous fight—with superior weapons against superior numbers—with the native, has taken more than his fair share of the land on which both the natives and he must live, and has left less than a fair share to the native. It is quite arguable that a European farmer might justly and with public advantage be allotted a larger share of land than a native, and that it must be fenced and natives excluded from it; and it would be neither necessary nor practical to contend for a readjustment that would provide for more than the reasonably considered needs of the native. Such a readjustment would leave the white community still in possession of a greatly disproportionate share.

A broadly just policy of redistribution would be to expropriate, at a cost to be paid for by a loan provision which should be charged on the

European community, at least the amount of land estimated (as by the Commissioners under the 1913 Act or other tribunals) to be required to make fair redress to the native community of the injustice inflicted upon them in the past, and that that land should be added to the native reserves either as communal tribal property or as native land administered by a Native Trust Department advised by Native Councils. Such a proposal, however, is obviously, in established political conditions, quite Utopian. Practical political controversy in this connection revolves, not around any question of restitution of rights to the native, or of attempting on a statesmanlike scheme of policy to redress injustice in the present distribution of property interests in the land— there is no idea of transferring gratuitously to the native community any equivalent of what the European acquired gratuitously at its expense, or even of transferring it at what it may have cost the present holders. Positively the storm of immediate controversy rages over no more far-reaching question of justice to natives than whether they shall be allowed to retain former rights (now suspended) or any substitute for them —that is, to acquire any land at all, at any cost borne by themselves, anywhere outside of the overcrowded native reserves and locations into which European conquest has penned them. Europeans—"fighting an unequal fight against the native," but being in complete command of the Legislature and all the powers of Government—

were clamouring that the native should be deprived of this constitutional right by discriminatory legislation. General Botha tried to secure him in the partial retention of it, in certain districts, at the cost of being deprived of it in all the rest of the country. This would not have been an instalment of justice, even had it not been applied with the exasperating trickery which I shall now proceed to describe, entirely to the native's detriment; it would have been, at best, a further infliction of injustice, and the natives felt it as such. But it was not a large enough instalment of advantage over the native to Europeans to satisfy them, and General Hertzog has had to try again. No one can know better than General Hertzog the ridiculous futility of the Colour Bar Law he has passed as an attempt to avert the evils impending over South Africa by some kind of ostensible relaxation of the pressure of the "unequal fight against the native." But the Labour Party having got their bit against the native industrial workers, the other side of the Coalition must needs have theirs, in the form I am about to analyse, against the rural Kaffir. Which party in this coalition of cowardice and short-sighted self-seeking is (in the conscience of its more intelligent members) the more ashamed and distrustful of the policy of the other it would be difficult to conjecture.

CHAPTER XI

GENERAL HERTZOG'S EIRENICON TO THE NATIVE

WHEN the Government of South Africa was forcing through the Union Legislature the Colour Bar Law, which was passed, in May 1926, after two rejections in the Senate, by a majority in a joint sitting of the Senate and the Assembly, the Prime Minister, General Hertzog, explained that whatever disadvantages this law might impose upon natives, it ought to be viewed in conjunction with the compensating boons which the Government intended to confer on them by other parts of their complete native policy. The Bills framing this policy have since then been published. They include a Bill to amend the Natives Land Act, 1913, two Bills to amend the franchise laws and the Parliamentary representation of natives and coloured people, of which the most important provision is for the disfranchisement of natives in Cape Colony (to which I have briefly referred above), and one to establish a Union Native Council, to have powers to deal with such matters "affecting natives only" as Parliament may specifically prescribe—a commendable measure.

General Hertzog, in describing his intended native policy, made the following very definite and fair-spoken statement: "Provision must be made by Parliament by which the native will be placed in the position to become possessed of the further ground which was promised him under the Act of 1913." That Act was framed as a "segregation" measure. Native acquisitions of land among European holdings had created alarm. The Act intended that in addition to the existing native reserves and locations (which it confirmed) further areas should be prescribed in which natives and natives only should be allowed to buy or lease, and that native buying or leasing should be barred in all other parts of the Union, and existing native property in those parts and European property in the proposed native areas got rid of as far as possible by expropriation.

That was the announced policy. It was an ideal. Most people in South Africa with practical acquaintance with the facts of the situation recognised that, except at the cost of great disturbance, inconvenience, and injustice, any adequate compensation for which there was no prospect of getting provided, it would prove impracticable. Moreover, any genuine segregation policy which really did "place the native in a position to become possessed of the ground promised him under the Act" would have stampeded the farmers in alarm for their labour supply. The Beaumont Commission, appointed to prepare a detailed scheme for carrying out the Act, exceptionally qualified as it was, could only produce a report, the proposals of which were vehemently objected to by both Europeans and natives. A further batch of Commissions, to make fresh proposals with regard to the several Provinces, was appointed. This new Bill is the result of what they reported. Meanwhile, for the last thirteen years, the so-called "Natives Land Act" has been operative in those provisions which barred natives from getting any more land, and has remained only partially inoperative in those provisions which promised to say where they were to be allowed to get some. After these later Commissions had reported, the Government allowed certain purchases of land by natives in the proposed native areas; but they also allowed purchases of land in those areas, including Crown lands,[1] by Europeans.

"This Act," says Professor Jabavu,[2] "satisfied no one. The natives naturally objected to the restriction of their right to purchase, and the Europeans were unwilling to have their farms set aside for native occupation. Two Commissions were appointed to recommend the areas which should be selected, but their suggestions have not been accepted. The Act is now thirteen years old, but no additional areas have been opened for native occupation. On the contrary, the evictions of native tenants who have nowhere to go have been rigorously carried out by the farmers with harrowing results. . . . Of all

[1] My authority for this statement is only verbal, but from two responsible South Africans.

[2] M.A., London ; Professor of Bantu languages, Fort Hare College, S.A.

the grievances harboured by the natives against European rules the greatest is this Land Act." The European farmers and landholders have refused to part with an acre of land for increased native settlement. "They are solidly opposed to any scheme of segregation calculated to provide more land and independence for black men. . . . These farmers control the Government of the country. The belief of the white farmer is that additional land provided for the native will react detrimentally on their labour market."

Whether this apprehension is well or ill founded—and I myself believe it to be ill founded—the inference from it that the native must not be allowed to have land in his own country, but that any and every white man is entitled to have whatever land he wants and natives to work it, is impressive. And the native quite clearly apprehends its significance. His racial spokesmen leave us in no doubt about that.

"The black man," Professor Jabavu continues, "does not ask for much—only for justice— justice in land distribution, justice in economic opportunity, and justice in political representation. This is no excessive demand. There will never be any racial goodwill in the country until it is granted willingly by the authorities."

General Hertzog's eirenicon to the black man as a set-off to depriving him of economic opportunity and political representation is the effort he is making to do him justice in land distribution by his new Bill. He has assembled the farmers and told them that he must have ten million morgen (20,000,000 acres) made available for native purchase or lease. That is just about what the Beaumont Commission said was necessary for carrying out the 1913 Act eleven years ago; and it would do to start if there were any real probability of the land being made available, or of the natives who most need land being able to buy. But let us examine what the Bill offers. That such a Bill should be announced by the Prime Minister of the Union as "a satisfactory solution for the native as well as the white man," will be found illuminative as to the character of the axioms on the basis of which the South African Government's whole scheme of native policy is conceived.

The Bill removes in respect of scheduled areas, additional to the reserves and locations confirmed in the 1913 Act, the prohibition of native purchase or lease of land. Such areas are styled "Released Areas." But it releases each district only in favour of natives belonging to particular tribes. Members of such tribes may buy land in the districts specified as appointed for them. The educated Europeanised native, if he is to get any land, must go back into his tribal society. The detribalised native, urban or rural (there are 587,000 urban, partly from Reserves, and about 2,000,000 rural outside the Reserves), needs homestead land within reach of his place of employment on which to keep and bring up his family. The alternative is a deplorable black slum population.

But it is not possible for him to go back into his tribal society. He has become Europeanised. He has been taught that he has an individual soul, individual responsibilities, individual duties and rights in regard to his work and earning. He must therefore remain, on the one hand, landless, and, on the other, restricted by the Colour Bar Law to "Kaffir work" and the Kaffir unskilled pay, on which, without land, he and his family cannot live.

If a native is still a tribe member he may share in the use of such land as his tribe may be able to buy. Chiefs can buy land. They have to do so if they are to keep their tribe together, as they can no longer take it by force. The individual rural native may acquire such estates as out of his wages (of 4d. to 8d. a day and rations) he may be able to buy for himself at such price as a white owner, if willing to sell, may demand. The European is not, as the 1913 Act intended, excluded from buying in these "released" areas. He will be a competitor with the native, and will always have the preference, even if he does not bid higher, from a white vendor. It is clear that the purchase of land by individual natives for themselves cannot in general become a practical proposition. They are too poor. Occasional tribal purchases will doubtless take place, but it is obvious that the area of native-owned land cannot for many

years be materially increased by individual purchases; and the reserves and locations are overcrowded. The position is aggravated by the
provisions of the Bill as to fencing. These are
extremely drastic, much more so than those
applicable to Europeans under existing Union
law. There are further obstructive restrictions
on sales to natives of lands adjacent to white
men.

So much for the native who may acquire.
The Bill does not effectually provide, and there
exists no official agency for conducting the
acquisition of land by natives. Certain local
receipts, quite inadequate for any material purpose, are proposed to be set aside for a "Purchase
and Advances Fund." But it is necessary, if
this or any other such law is not to remain
practically inoperative, that a Native Land Trust
Department should be set up, acting through
Boards in each Province, with power to acquire
and redistribute land as well as to finance natives
who buy by direct dealings. Such a Department has been continually demanded by all who,
with any genuine desire to give the natives a
chance, have devoted even the most perfunctory
consideration to the essential prerequisites for
so doing. Without it the native is not "placed
in the position to become possessed of the land
promised him." The would-be native purchaser
or lessee of land is set an obstacle race. A tribe
may deal collectively, but no other association
of natives may do so except under special regula-

tions not defined. Funds must be provided to enable the Department to purchase estates and retail them to native applicants. Loans would be necessary, to be repaid by instalments. Borrowing powers up to £1,000,000 ought to be obtained by the Government for this purpose. Settlement should be guided and agricultural progress stimulated. The method is already familiar.

Now let us look at that side of the Bill which is to be "satisfactory to the white man." The Governor-General *may*, and on the application of not less than one-half of the *white* population in any district *shall*, proclaim that within such district no native shall reside upon land unless—

(*a*) he is the registered owner of such land ; or

(*b*) he is a servant under the provisions of the Masters and Servants Law (enforcible by penal sanctions) ; or

(*c*) he is licensed as a "labour tenant"—in which case he and any dependent of his above eighteen years of age are also to be deemed "servants."

(A labour tenant has to do at least 180 days' work in the year for his master as rent for his holding. Since 1909 the customary obligation for such tenancies has been 90 days) ; or

(*d*) he is licensed as a squatter for which he (nominally his landlord) is to pay an annual license fee of from £3 to £5 for his continuing to reside on the land that belonged to his people before the European annexed it. The intention is that the squatter shall be got rid of. He must either get off or get under. Leave the land—and where is he to get off it to?—or become a labour tenant.

The designation "squatter," to anyone unfamiliar with the foundations of South African land economy, would suggest a class of trespassers intrusively established in irregular occupancy on other persons' land. It usually means, however, in that environment, precisely the reverse. It means a native whose land the white man has by the divine right of his whiteness appropriated as his own, and from which he has not been able or found it convenient to attempt to expel the resident native. As a consideration for his tolerance he exacts from him rent, averaging £2 a year per adult male, and, if possible, induces or compels him when required to work for him. The squatter's tenure has its origin in white landgrabbing: it is demoralising and increasingly inconvenient to the improving landowner. To the idler or absentee and to the speculative land companies it provides an unearned income. It is progressively destructive, oppressive, and degrading to the natives subjected to it. South African Governments have desired to eliminate it and have legislated to restrain it. The laws have been ignored. There are said to be about 300,000 squatters in the Transvaal alone.

Mr E. L. Matthews, the Union Government's law adviser (the legal mind often seems to be somewhat deficient in political delicacy) reported on the Act of 1913: "It is in the Transvaal that the squatting evil has existed to the greatest extent. It is impossible to dispossess these squatters, many of whom or their progenitors have been on the land from time immemorial. It is doubtful if the law could be enforced against the principal offenders—the Land Companies. Squatters are a profitable asset to the Land Companies and other owners. If the laws were enforced large numbers of natives would be dispossessed and have nowhere to go."

General Hertzog's Bill offers them a way of escape. They may have a chance of becoming "labour tenants."

The intention of the high squatters' licence duty is to kill out the class. If a squatter dies or removes, he may not be replaced by another squatter. The licensing fees payable by an employer of labour tenants are to increase rapidly in amount with the number licensed to him: the demand for squeezed-out squatters as labour tenants will thus be discouraged. Where are these people to get to? and what value will they be able to realise for their cattle when they have them on their hands without land to support them? They can only become common labourers.

The contemplated tax of £3 to £5 a year on squatters, on the top of their present rents, which hundreds of thousands of them would be simply unable to pay, would be under any circumstances a grossly unjust, oppressive, and indefensible class impost. Under the existing circumstances of the native in regard to land-rights, which I have described, it is barefacedly brutal. Imagine any statesman in any other country in the whole of the modern world proposing such a tax on the poorest part of his country's peasantry! And this peasantry are among the poorest in all the world. As labourers they can earn about 6d. a day. General Hertzog proposes it without turning a hair. It does not occur to him that there is anything remarkable in the idea. That is what is wrong with South Africa. The native has no rights. He may be taxed and pushed about as any white man's Government thinks desirable. General Hertzog would not, presumably, have dealt with the Irish land question by putting a crushing tax on all tenancies. If squatter tenancy is a bad system (and it is,—as the Irish tenancies were) it should be superseded by similar methods; the landowners expropriated and the native peasantry settled as tenants or tax-paying freeholders under the Government. If the tax is imposed and the landlords cannot pass it on, as in most cases it will be impossible for them to do, or if they try to do so and fail, what is going to be done to probably at least a quarter of a million squatters who will not pay more rent than they are now doing, and will have nowhere to move to? It will be very interesting to see— so interesting that the experiment may be worth making. You cannot move these masses of natives suddenly into either labour tenancies or farm service, nor can you—even if they could find and buy land—move such a population suddenly on to new land which they would have to bring into cultivation. How could they live while they were getting their new land into working, fencing, and finding water for their stock, building houses? Are they to be moved from the high veld where they have been bred to the low veld where the climate and cultivation are quite different? Masses of them would simply have to sit tight and not pay. All these practical considerations appear to have been blandly ignored—but that is not my concern in this Anatomy. I merely desire to point out the characteristics of that traditional mentality which the aseptic air of the illimitable veld has preserved untainted since the forgotten times of slavery. "*Quid-quid delirant reges plectantur Abanti.*" If you have white mining trouble—colour bar the native. If white men don't turn off the natives they find on the land they have taken—harry the blacks. And General Hertzog is so obviously well-intentioned.

The licenses for labour tenants are to be granted by a Divisional Council or Board, which will of course consist of the local white farmers, and which is to distribute such licenses according solely to the labour requirements of the applicant employers. The labour tenant will have no say in the choice of his master, who may be changed at the end of any year. There is no provision for his interest, if so displaced, in unexhausted values on his holding.

The squatter, then, is to be driven off or,

apparently, blown away into the air. The labour tenant will be forced more and more to become merely a servant. As a servant he cannot save enough money to buy himself land. If he migrates to the town he is to meet the colour-bar, cannot earn a sufficient wage to maintain himself and his family, and has to house them in detrimental conditions.

This part of the Bill discloses the inducements whereby General Hertzog hopes to get some land released by the landowning and farming class that has burked the 1913 Act and kept it a dead letter. They are to have an increased forced supply of bonded labourers, and their families under similar obligation. And the natives they do not want as servants are to be forced off the land of their birth with the derisory alternative of finding a bit of it they can buy. The 1913 Act purported to rest on a segregation policy. There is no segregation policy in this Bill. It allows a certain speckling of native ownership to be set up among white men by such natives as can afford to buy and establishes all those who cannot—or, at any rate, as many of them as are wanted, as bondsmen and bondswomen on the Europeans' surrounding lands.

The schedules in the Bill of areas to be released do not give information of their extent, from which their adequacy could be judged. The powers given in the 1913 Act to the Government to increase native areas are repealed. Substitutions are allowed; but the maximum is not to exceed the total recommended by the Provincial Land Commissions under the 1913 Act, which were set up after the fiasco of the Beaumont Commission. If the provisions forbidding residence of natives except under the conditions I have related are enacted, all former estimates of the areas required by the natives must be exceeded; for there will rapidly be created an immense body of natives faced with the alternative of seeking land (at impossible prices) on inadequate areas or becoming servants of European masters. To be out of work will mean to be homeless—and for a native to be homeless in a proclaimed district is forbidden by the Bill. General Smuts is reported (*Times*, 27th September 1926) as saying that "the 'white' towns would be flooded with rural natives forced off them by the drastic licensing system proposed by the Government."

This, then, is General Hertzog's eirenicon to the natives, his agrarian compensation for the Industrial Colour Bar Law.

No wonder if the native finds the white man's proceedings an inexhaustible joke. General Botha, with generously impassioned words on behalf of his rights, passes a law, which is called "The Natives' Land Law," which puts a stopper on the native getting land as he could before, and keeps it on from 1913 to this day. General Hertzog, to give him "his rights in the land of his birth," produces a Bill to "amend" the Land Law. And its provisions for the native's land-rights and

117

for his right conditions of living are as above set forth. How can the natives be angry with such pathetically topsy-turvy philanthropists, standing on their own heads to look at his world. The title of the "Charity Organisation" Society pales the brilliancy of its humour beside these gems of ironic nomenclature.

CHAPTER XII

LAND AND THE POOR WHITE

THERE is a good deal of land in South Africa which, without the provision of water by storage or boring, is practically uninhabitable. Other districts need drainage. The European has the ability, which the native has not, to make parts of such land habitable both by Europeans and natives. If by their own knowledge, the investment of their own capital, and the application of their own labour Europeans should make such land habitable by Europeans, and should not want to employ natives to help them to make and keep it so, no one could regard natives as having any equitable claim to the use of such improved land. But if Europeans cannot create productive estates in this manner without natives to do the manual labour, and do not contemplate using them without employing natives, the conditions which inevitably and automatically undermine the ideal of segregation are introduced at the very outset, even in areas which could not become habitable for a settled native population unless the European takes in hand the task of making them so. It is the instinct of the white man (in accordance with the characteristic process of capitalist economy), wherever he has in such a manner developed new areas, to establish himself in the position of a permanent exploiter of the native by retaining the private ownership of the land and reaping the whole of the rent and profit that can be extracted from it, keeping the native dependent and under control by allowing him no land to be directly worked for himself, and thus to keep him subservient as a tied labourer unable to improve his own position. In so doing, in such areas as I have supposed to have been made habitable by his own initiative, the European is, of course, proceeding strictly in accordance with the accepted conventional ethics of his own civilisation; he is merely acting as European landowners do and as they have acted for centuries. It cannot, at best, be considered an amiable system. In Europe it has long been discredited. In England so completely so, that the Liberal Party believe that if they attack it the constituencies will return them once more to power. South African landed interests will no doubt maintain it as long as they can. In South Africa the landowning class being white, and having the political franchise, whereas the proletariat is predominantly black and has not, there is at present little effective political movement against landlordism. The only effectual argument against it there is likely to be, not its oppressive character, but the inevitably increasing inconvenience of its reactions on racial relations, which South African Europeans are already seeking expedients to mitigate without sacrificing the economic ideals on which individualist land-lordism and capitalism rest—the ideal of getting all you can, as long as you can, out of fellow human beings whom you have at a disadvantage, and taking all possible steps to keep them as long as possible at the greatest possible dis-advantage. South African native policy is just now devoting special attention to this latter purpose, the system having begun to show ominous symptoms or promises of working un-healthily for the European, and of needing clamping and strapping up; just as in England, where Trade Unionism is going to be tackled and put in its place by the Conservative Government.

So much for any hypothetical areas in which the white man might claim the credit of having initiated the creation of economic value in land. Johannesburg and the whole of the mining dis-tricts might be put in this same class. In other areas, where it would have been quite possible for the native to maintain himself on his own economic methods, if only the European had not imperilled his water-supply by tampering with his rain-making institutions and his land-supply by preventing him from evicting his neighbours, and by reducing his rate of mortality, the recognition that the Anglo-Dutchman in South Africa has merely behaved in a crudely barbarous fashion, precisely as did his low-German ancestors in the dark ages in their Northern invasions, in appropriating the lands

121

of natives and making those who remained on them their bondsmen, gains ground more easily. And there have never been lacking in South Africa continuous protests against European dealings with natives purely on the ground that these dealings were unjust, barbarous, and uncivilised, inhumane to the natives, and dishonourable and disastrous to Christian and intelligent Europeans. The Europeans in South Africa, it cannot be too often repeated, until the recognition of the fact—acknowledged by many among them, including responsible statesmen—is made a basis for active agrarian policy, have dealt unjustly with the native in regard to the distribution of land of which the white man has not created the value, and owe a debt of readjustment of property in habitable agricultural land. But more important than the physical distribution of the actual possession and control of landed property is the recognition that the belief that relations between Europeans and natives can be so regulated by conditions of land holding and employment as to keep the interests of the races separate, is an illusion. A white man, merely as landowner and master, cannot employ natives, without the interests of the native affecting and reacting upon his own. European society cannot, as the repressionist school of policy vainly imagines, exploit native society without being undermined. This truth is obvious and familiar enough to most moderately intelligent South Africans, and I need not labour it. The Economic Commission lucidly and patiently does so, and its Report may, it is to be hoped, effect some further penetration of the obstinately conservative intelligence of the repressionist party.

The problem of the Poor White in its special South African features is a by-product of the dealings of the European with the native since the abolition of slavery (1) in regard to land, and (2) in regard to his position in relation to the white, as a labourer. The sins of the fathers are being visited upon this third generation, and will be upon the fourth. The destitution of education which the conditions of the pastoral settlement rendered prevalent has co-operated to his demoralisation. South African Governments have adopted and seek to pursue intelligent and enlightened policies in aid of white men's farming. There has been no lack of sufficient appreciation amongst their available counsellors as to what things are wanted and what, with goodwill, may be done. The farmers, Sir Horace Plunkett has told us, do not take so much advantage of the facilities already established by the State as they might. Governments have also adopted a sound and liberal policy in their endeavour to mitigate the Poor White problem, by enabling landless Europeans to acquire land. There is unsatisfied white land-hunger alongside the native need for more land. In 1925, for 12 farms of 150 morgen (about 300 acres), each in the Orange Free State, there were 800 applicants. The Economic Commission deal fully and luminously with this line of policy. They challenge the evil of land monopoly as it affects the whites. The restrictions, they say, of the landowners' as distinct from the land-users' share of the produce of industry on the land, "to the smallest possible amount, is a matter which requires the urgent attention of the Government." As to settlement, "the sum of £400,000 which was provided by Parliament for loans to settlers in 1925 was expended in the first five months of the year. A great deal is being done under Government Land Settlement Schemes to enable men to acquire plots of land for themselves." But "when the Government enters the field as a purchaser for land settlement it automatically sends up the price of land. . . . It is essential that steps should be taken to prevent landowners holding up settlers in this way to the ransom of increasing prices."

Quite so. Here is, at any rate, a means of rehabilitation for many Poor Whites—for there is plenty of land—provided, at any rate, they are prepared to work for themselves. The policy indicated is obvious—South Africa must do as New Zealand had to do with her pre-emptors of large landholdings. It is only a question whether the South African Government is likely to be any better able than any other Government dependent on the votes of landowners to pursue it. Obviously too, as the parties now in power are so anxious for segregation, and so much in love with the colour bar, the Government should, in any provision of land for white settlers which they finance and control, stipulate that no Kaffirs should be employed by them, or should prescribe a minimum wage, adequate for a white man or for any agricultural labour employed on these farms. They will thus do good in two ways, they will provide the Poor White with land, and they will prevent these farms at least from breeding fresh trouble through the infection of the slavery-bred system of Kaffir work and wages that is destroying South Africa.

And what they recognise as necessary to be done for the Poor White, they must also recognise as necessary to be done for the landless native; and more liberally, because they are very heavily in the natives' debt in this matter. "A considerable addition," say the Economic Commissioners, "to the inadequate areas reserved at present for natives is *the first essential* towards a reasonable solution of the problems raised by the contact of the native with European civilisation." The Europeans must find means to agree quickly with this adversary with whom they have to wage their "unequal fight." That is "the first essential" to the reasonable solution of their problem. The penalty, if they fail to do so, will surely become stiffer the longer this debt accumulates. It is already, as all South Africa is beginning to recognise, serious enough. That, however, is an internal problem. What the rest

125

of the world is directly and deeply concerned with is to take care that the principles of European dealing with Africans which have created South Africa's difficulties are repressed outside the South African Union, if they should be clung to within its boundaries, and that they are prevented from spreading further. Swaziland and Bechuanaland must obviously be kept outside the Union. Experience has demonstrated that it is not enough for the Imperial Government, in transferring responsibility to the Union Government, to attempt to safeguard the essential rights of natives or Asiatics. Assurances are liable to be repudiated and established rights to be annulled by anti-native or anti-Asiatic enactments at the dictates of electoral expediency, on any demand of the European electors who monopolise political power, in fear for their own supposed economic interests or their usurped privileges. It is permissible to hope that the plague of South African and capitalist native policy has been stayed in Kenya—though it remains to be seen whether, when the "White Defence Force" now being enrolled there is sufficiently organised, the British Government will be prepared to stand up against reactionary demands on behalf of the Europeans any more stiffly than they did against the hasty conscription of filibusters that was organised to intimidate them, with the threat of seizing the Government, during the controversy about Indian rights in 1923. Southern Rhodesia, too, whose Government is both liberally inspired and anxious to avoid all risk of the Nemesis that is threatening her neighbours south of the Crocodile River may be expected to maintain a frontier for traditional European principles.

CHAPTER XIII

RACIAL DISCRIMINATION

THE "Colour Bar" Law which was passed in May
1926 by a majority in a joint session of the Senate
and the House of Assembly, after having twice
been rejected by the Senate, purports to amend
the Mines and Works Act of 1911, upon the plea
that some amendment was necessary to enable a
discrimination to be validly made which, when
it was attempted previously under that Act, was
declared by the Courts of the Transvaal to be
illegal. The Mines and Works Act, 1911, had
empowered the Minister for Mines and Industries
to require that persons employed in and about
mines, works, and machinery should be in possession of certificates of competency. In the
exercise of what he considered to be his power
under that law the Minister had made a regulation prescribing that no native or Asiatic should
be allowed to be employed in or about mines,
works, or machinery.

An action at law was brought against an employer named Hildick-Smith, on the ground that
he had employed a native who—it was admitted
in evidence—was perfectly qualified to drive an
engine. The case was dismissed by the magistrate, who opined that no person could be declared
not qualified to receive a certificate of competency

to run machines simply because he had a black skin, and held that the regulation was _ultra vires_. The Attorney-General, on behalf of the Crown in South Africa, appealed to the High Court, and the Bench of four judges upheld the decision of the magistrate. There is an interesting passage in the judgment of one of the judges, Mr Krause, which I will quote:

"It is remarkable that one of the oldest laws of the Transvaal dealing with the native population recognises the fact that 'the ignorance, usages, and customs of the native population render them unfit for the duties and responsibilities of civilised life.' However, in providing for their better treatment and management by placing them under special supervision, the lawgiver expresses the desire that the differentiation shall only continue to exist 'until they shall be able to properly understand and appreciate such duties and responsibilities as they may reasonably be deemed capable of performing in obedience to the general law.' The law contains no provision restricting or prohibiting the native from competing with the white man"—which is the sole and simple reason for this Colour Bar Law—"or debarring him from following any trade or occupation he pleases; in fact, the policy of the Statute seems to contemplate his gradual emancipation, and seeks to encourage and educate him 'to understand and appreciate the duties and responsibilities of civilised life.'

"The policy of the regulation, on the contrary,

deprives the native from enjoying the very fruits of his advancement, by prohibiting him from performing such work as in this case it was proved he was capable of doing. Greater repugnancy to the principles of the Statute can hardly be imagined."

The new law, if its powers are acted upon, which General Hertzog has said it is not yet intended should fully be done, will bring it about that no native or Asiatic would be "deemed competent" or be allowed to be employed in any mines, works, or industries in which any kind of mechanical propulsion is employed. They might not be employed in brick-works, in lime-works, or sugar mills. They would not be allowed to make use of their faculties to obtain the benefits of any kind of technical education or advancement, in order that they may be kept down as an unskilled proletariat. That is the whole intention of the legislation now being supported by the South African Government and by what so quaintly calls itself the "Labour Party of South Africa": all South African labourers being black.

In this commentary I keep on the surface; I survey only the overt actions of Europeans in South Africa in their dealings with natives; political and economic proceedings of whose equitable aspects according to normal European standards of decent human behaviour and of whose inevitable reactions on the sensibilities, temper, judgment, and accumulating resolve of a growing multitude of vigorous and spirited human beings, any intelligent person who realises what has been and is being done can form but one judgment. I do not wish to inflame animosities and prejudices by attempting to exhibit the whole temperamental truth of the situation, or by illustrating the manner in which ill-conditioned Europeans act and speak towards natives and Asiatics. The symptoms of the brand of mental deficiency known as negrophobia are familiar enough. I confine myself to the shortcomings of normally intelligent and decent-minded people. Mr Maurice Evans, a most temperate, conservative and profoundly perspicacious witness, set forth, sixteen years ago, sufficient material [1] for an understanding of the position as it manifestly was even then; and the facts of it are immeasurably more obvious and significant now. A letter from a South African author of well-known name is before me as I write. He says: "The attitude of the colonists is absolutely suicidal. They rely solely on machine guns for their supremacy. All the labour of the country is performed by natives: the whites are degenerating very quickly; they have been morally defeated by the native's power of suffering, by his tenacity of life, and lastly but most importantly, of the black man's sense of humour." (Mr Evans makes a similar reference to the amused astonishment at the white man's proceedings and pretensions which constantly turns provocations to bitterness into inimitably ludi-

[1] *Black and White in South-East Africa.*

131

crous comedy for the black man.) "It is by his sense of humour that the native dominates the country morally. Of course in Natal we have the Zulu strain, which is by far the most aristocratic of Bantu tribes. They still retain a considerable amount of their military prestige, unfortunately, which may end things badly for them; but if they rely on the fine qualities that I have enumerated they will more than hold their own." . . . These extracts are from a private letter which says a good deal more in illustration. And, presumably, General Smuts knew what he was talking about when he said publicly, on the South African situation, with regard to the Anti-Indian Bill:

"We shall gather on our heads the hatred of the whole of Asia. We shall feel the weight of that hatred in the years to come. The Bill will be taken as an outrage not only by Black Africa but by Yellow Asia. We, a handful of whites, are ring-fencing ourselves, first with an inner ring of black hatred and, beyond that, with a ring of hatred of the whole of Asia, for while only a few Asiatics are directly affected by this Bill, the inclusion of their name will win us the hatred of hundreds of millions of Asiatics from the north of Asia to the south." And again, on the Colour Bar Bill:

"A year ago I warned the Union Government that the effects of their policy would not stop in South Africa but would provoke a world's conflict.

"An extension of the colour bar at this moment, when the Prime Minister is on the point of bringing forward a new native policy, would be disastrous. . . . Native opinion is largely in revolt. The natives are seething with discontent all over South Africa. . . . It is not only the natives who are making difficulties. There is no doubt that when the Asiatic Bill is passed then the trouble will begin. We know it is coming. The Asiatic Bill must lead to the gravest troubles of administration. I knew that in 1924. . . . It is inevitable. In these circumstances the Colour Bar Bill, gratuitously produced here, is a firebrand flung into a haystack."

The *principle* of the colour bar, now newly established in the law of the South African Union, is, and has long been, in practical operation there, though its application has been accentuated of late years. Its basis is that of the Boer denial of "equality in Church or State," but more practically, perhaps, the fact that the native was mostly unskilled and ignorant of European arts, and that for generations no one but the missionaries ever dreamed of educating him, or apparently of imagining that he could be educated. The Cape coloured people did get European education, and they have kept on the right side of the economic colour bar because they found employment naturally in the technical manual trades as the community of which they were begotten developed. It is observable that what may strictly be called colour prejudice or even race prejudice

has been until comparatively recently less acrimonious and vicious in its temper in much of
South Africa than it was two generations ago
in the West Indies or is in the Southern States of
America. The ordinary white South African
has not, until he began to feel his competition as
a wage-worker, detested or even despised the
native as the white West Indian used to (and still
does in some islands) the coloured man, or so
much as the white West Indian or American
Southerner did the emancipated negro.

In the Cape and Natal there were Europeans
and there were Kaffir boys, and they got on fairly
well together and served each other's convenience,
with many causes of grumbling and dissatisfaction,
no doubt, but on the whole without hostility
or ill-feeling. The African, whether Negro or
Bantu, is so remarkably easy to get on with
pleasantly if you deal with him decently. He is
often madly irritating as an employee, but if
his understanding is more limited, his temper is
much better and his judgment much cooler than
that of the average white man. He is quite prepared to be stiffly dealt with when he has been
trying to take advantage or has transgressed
obligations he recognises. He is submissive to
force and does not resent its application if it has
a recognisable basis of status, reason, or equity.
His tribal civilisation, with its violent sanctions,
has taught him that. That is why he is deemed
servile when he is under authority (because he
puts up with oppression he cannot defeat), but

impudent when he acts in a natural manner on the white man's conventions of independence and self-respect. And he is affectionate and good-humoured. The colour bar rests on a theory of unchangeable social status or caste. It has some superficial similarities with the caste bar in India, based also originally on colour and racial conquest; and so long as the system of money contract did not infringe the system of status it was workable. But it is essentially incompatible with a contractual civilisation and the introduction of the capitalist industrial economy. That system implies the right of bargaining for one's labour contract, and making the best one can of whatever capacities one may have to sell. When the capitalist employer comes on the scene, making discrimination as to the labour force he must employ for particular work in order to make his profits, which it is the law of his activity to do, then, and not till then, antagonism is introduced between the newly-created wage-working proletarian white and the native—who, in regard to the qualifications which properly determine wage contracts, are on exactly the same footing, and must be compared according to economic values. The native African, everywhere, has a very keen and direct apprehension of equity, and if you take your relations with him out of the sphere of status into that of contract, he will very promptly recognise any injustice of your dealings with him in that category and will resent it. It is one thing that he should come in and out of his reserves as

135

a tribal native and do Kaffir boy's work for white
farmers or housekeepers on the customary hap-
hazard basis, and at a conventional standard rate
of pay and ration, but quite another that, when
an employer wants work which he can do as well
as a white man, because white men have detribalised him and taught him in the mission school
or in the mines to do it, his qualifications for doing
it should be judged of by any standard except that
of the white man's valuation of that kind of skill.
Much more so when, as is often the case in the
mines, he himself has taught the tenderfoot white
his job.

The old agricultural system of the Boers and
the habits and point of view which British immigrants partly acquired from them in connection
with it, were comparatively innocuous and in-
offensive. The Boers declared that they would
not allow the black man social equality or political
rights, and they had, as I have pointed out, some
reason for doing so; but as Mr Justice Krause
pointed out in the Hildick-Smith case, their law
did not assert that he was incapable of improvement, nor did their Constitution embody any
prohibition against his employment in tasks he
was fitted for. Nor did the voortrekkers appropriate more land to the detriment of the native
than they wanted for their own patriarchal farms.
But the commercialised South African of the
capitalising period has taken away all the land of
which he could dispossess the native; not to use,
but to hold for unearned increment, and to keep

the native wages down, and now forbids the native by law to enjoy the emoluments of the civilisation whose conditions he has imposed on him and which he has founded and is building up on his underpaid labour.

The stoicism of the African native is notable. What answers among his tribes to our public school education is specially addressed to teaching him to endure pain and provocation without showing it. If the black man were insensible to pain and discomfort, as some white men sometimes assert and more seem to assume, the special attention paid to this Spartan discipline would be superfluous. It would be very comfortable to believe that it extinguishes sensibility. The African submits to manifestly superior force, recognising necessity, and is patient. But he remains alive, and the Bantu in South Africa remain prolific and vigorous in spite of white men's diseases. The West Indian slave, anticipating Einstein's transfusion of the categories, made a proverb: "Time longer dan Rope." That might well be taken as the motto of Africanism.

It is really the competition for wage-employment, the peculiar and characteristic product of the capitalist system, that is chiefly responsible for poisoning the relations between white men and natives and bringing this colour bar programme into politics. That being so, it has become more obviously expedient than it was when the Cape Constitution was framed that the natives should be barred from political power. They might start

a real "Labour Party." General Hertzog therefore announced in November 1925:

> "It is clear to me that the other three
> provinces cannot permit the native franchise
> to be extended on the Cape basis; neither
> can the native be given the right to become
> a Member of Parliament. It is clear, further,
> that the grant of the franchise to the natives
> on the Cape basis *would necessarily* mean the
> ruin of the white population and of European
> civilisation in the Union. . . . It must be
> patent to all that the Cape native franchise
> must be fundamentally altered unless we
> want to see either civil war or the white
> man's ruin and that of European civilisation
> in South Africa."

Professor Jabavu, speaking responsibly and as
a conciliator, explains to us that the Europeans
in the three northern provinces (Natal, Orange
Free State, Transvaal) really fear that the black
man, given equal opportunity to rise economically
and industrially, will eventually overwhelm the
white man and destroy his civilisation. In what
manner or why, if Europeans can persuade themselves to act sanely, it is conceived by intelligent
men that this disaster will come about, except on
the assumption that all white men are going to
become wage-earners and their work be taken
away from them by employers in favour of Kaffirs,
I find it difficult plausibly to imagine. If that is

indeed likely to happen, it will be the Europeans' own fault, the reward of his past dealings with the Kaffirs and of more indefensible future dealings, such as are now being threatened or called for. But as to the destruction of civilisation by any other process, white civilisation, according to my observation, is strong enough to take care of itself. If the black man is admitted to it he adopts it, and does not attempt or desire to overthrow it. He has not, like the Indian, an ancient civilisation of his own. Only if white civilisation destroys and deteriorates him will he destroy and deteriorate it. Certainly white civilisation, as it has dealt with the South African black man, has every ground for a bad conscience and for alarm. If Bolshevik missionaries preached their familiar indictment of capitalist European civilisation to South African natives, the latter could hardly fail already to recognise its close applicability, and to accept the moral that that civilisation must be destroyed, and it cannot be disputed that if capitalist industrialism is allowed to run riot in South Africa it will doubtless there produce the same results in unemployment as it does in European countries.

In the Cape Colony there never has been such a fear; the black and coloured man there was, from the time of Sir George Grey, allowed opportunity to rise in industry and politics, and yet the white man has never been threatened with submersion, absorption, or extinction. But as a result of the Union with the Boer republics and of the antagonisms created by the mining industry and the appearances on the scene of a Poor White proletariat the temper of public policy has undoubtedly been unbalanced, and even the Cape natives are now losing confidence in the beneficent tutelage of British institutions. There are 2,000,000 detribalised natives mixed up with the white agricultural community, and more than half a million such in urban areas. "The majority of whites in South Africa, especially the backvelders," says Dr Jabavu, "cling to the repressive policy, or else remain utterly indifferent to the whole problem. The policy has been historically proved wrong, unjust, and bad. It has produced an anti-white generation of natives, it has perpetrated the worst forms of legal injustice, produced ugly racial collisions and a spirit of racial animosity."

CHAPTER XIV

COLOUR WAR

IT is not within the intention of this Anatomy to suggest advice to South Africa as to how she should deal with her domestic difficulties. There are thousands of citizens of the Union—forming, indeed, probably a majority in locally recognised civic and intellectual distinction although at this moment a minority in political power—who know and have pointed out, far more fully and acutely than I have attempted to illuminate them, the fundamental causes of those difficulties. It is from South African writings and public utterances that I entirely draw the materials and the references to authorities reputed there which justify the analysis I am making. There is nothing that one would expect to be felt and recognised by any civilised Englishman, acquainted with the history of the relations of his own people with other races —African or Asiatic—and of the campaign of the human spirit against slavery, that is not, quite obviously and uncompromisingly, felt and recognised about South Africa by such South Africans. It would be astonishing if it were not so. Those, and the successors of those, who, in the face of dull-witted opposition, have worked in South Africa by far-seeing and humane methods to mitigate and overcome the difficulties of the inter-

141

actions of European and native, are abundantly qualified—if they can exercise the influence and the power—to guide her future development on even wiser lines.

But South Africa is by no means the only part of the world that is directly concerned in the prudent and equitable handling and reform of the disordered complication of her economic and interracial conditions, or entitled to form and express judgments and declare an attitude in respect of them.

I shall say but little about the policy of injustice and oppression that has been adopted by the Union Government against its citizens of Indian descent, settled there under promise that they should not be subjected to any discrimination founded on race, religion, or colour. That threat is, at the moment at which I write, suspended. The Government of India is to have time to defend the rights of its racials in formal conference with Ministers of the Union.

The Christian Church is damagingly wounded in the house of its friends by the Colour Bar Law. As reported in the *Cape Times* of the 7th May 1926, just prior to the joint meeting of the Senate and House of Assembly in which that law was carried, "a more representative protest than any made to the Prime Minister of the Union during recent years" was sent to General Hertzog in his capacity of Prime Minister, "expressing dissent from the terms of what is generally known as the Colour Bar Bill." This

protest was signed by the Archbishop of Cape-
town and all the Anglican Bishops in South
Africa; by the Councils or other representative
bodies of the Wesleyan, Unitarian, Baptist, Jewish,
Presbyterian, and Congregationalist communions;
by the Rev. J. Duplessis, Professor of Theology,
Dutch Reformed Church; by the committee of
joint Native Welfare Societies, and many other
persons of public distinction, missionaries, and
native representatives. Its condensed but perfectly accurate reference to the effect of the Bill
provoked a remarkable outburst of emotion (the
Cape Times called it "hysterical") from General
Hertzog in the debate of the joint sitting of the
two Houses upon it. "A more unworthy docu-
ment," he said, "by responsible, highly responsible, people has not seen the light of day in
connection with a matter like this for a hundred
years, when the Boers on the eastern borders were
slandered and driven out of the country by a
number of missionaries and others." He flatly
charged the signers of the memorial with lying,
vilifying, and slandering, reminded his hearers that
"the people of South Africa" had long "looked
on the missionaries of South Africa as a contemptible class of persons who should not be here,"
and warned the collection of spokesmen of the
religious communities represented, that "the
same sort of feeling may be aroused again by
circumstances which we cannot foresee to-day."
This uncensored explosion of the distress of
ancient grievances was obviously touched off

143

by the Prime Minister's misreading into the words of the memorial an imputation which they did not contain or justify, namely, that the instigating motive of his Bill was "colour prejudice." The ebullition deserves this reference only because it led General Hertzog to restate his actual motives, and the restatement, set over against the text of the memorial, which it does not, in fact, in the least degree refute or controvert, is exceedingly illuminating and instructive. The Prime Minister protested:—

> "My real reason why this Bill must go through is this: The Government is no longer going to sit down passively and allow of the possibility of a repetition of the strike and the conditions of 1922–23 and of the consequences thereof. The white man in South Africa has to fight an unequal fight [1] against the natives of South Africa, and if we do not take the necessary precautions to see the inequality and competition existing between the two are placed on such a footing that there is room for the native as well as the European, then not only will the strike and bloodshed of 1922 be repeated, but other things will be repeated in South Africa of a much more serious nature."

Those are General Hertzog's words as reported

[1] That, doubtless, is why the Administrator of Mandated South-West Africa bombed the Bondelswaart Hottentots from aeroplanes when they murmured against their Dog Tax.

in the *Cape Times*. Possibly misreporting may be responsible for some apparent confusion of meaning in them. Or it may perhaps be explained by the manifest agitation under which he was labouring. The strike of 1922–23 was a strike of white miners, "fighting an unequal fight," at wages of 10 to 1—I have set forth the position above—"against the natives," demanding that they should no longer be allowed to sharpen drills. They subsequently demanded the Colour Bar Law, and, in order to prevent a renewal of trouble in the mines, General Hertzog opined they must have it. In his judgment, apparently, it will place the inequality and competition between the two on such a footing that there will be "room for the native as well as the European": that is to say, that there will be room for the white man to continue to ride, in the time-honoured South African fashion, on the black man's back. The Economic Commission and every one of a long series of similar Commissions have reported that colour bar legislation is not likely to effect the results which General Hertzog, ostensibly, assumes are to be expected from it. But what the signers of the memorial, which he denounced as lying, vilificatory, and slanderous, actually said was, that they would leave economic and legal considerations aside, to be argued by others, as they have been by such Economic Commissions, but that they, as Christians, considered it "certainly wrong that any man should be legally prohibited from doing any kind of work for which he is qualified, merely on the ground of colour." It might be cavilled that the Bill discriminated not by "colour" but by descent, *i.e.* against all persons falling within its involved and arbitrary definition of a "native," but such a quibble was not the basis of General Hertzog's indignation. The measure is currently spoken of as "*the Colour Bar Law*." The memorialists, in effect, said: "It is contrary to the moral and religious principles of white civilisation and Christianity to discriminate as this Bill does against working men on the ground that they are 'natives' as therein defined." General Hertzog, instead of answering that these gentlemen's opinion was ignorant, that they were not qualified judges of right and wrong, morality, or religious principle, and that the Dutch Reformed Churches, whose representatives (except Dr Duplessis and a few other individuals) had not signed the memorial, were better authorities on these questions and presumably, as they kept silence, did not condemn it, lost his temper and accused them of charging him with acting on the ground of race prejudice, whereas he was, in fact, acting solely on grounds of political expediency, and merely "taking precautions" to please his white supporters by keeping the native in his proper place. In effect—and this is the only substantial point involved in this tempestuous incident— he maintains that a legal enactment debarring certain wage-workers from improving their position in their own country, on the ground of their racial origin, and their restriction to the permanent status of unskilled, underpaid labourers on the same ground, is legitimate, in order to enable other wage-workers, because they are of a different race, to maintain a highly privileged position on the footing of the natives' continued exploitation. I have already sufficiently justified this explanation of the native's position by the evidence of South Africans of specially selected qualifications and unimpeachable patriotism. Certainly, obviously, those were General Hertzog's motives of policy, and if anyone had suggested, as the memorialists did not, that he was merely indulging "colour prejudice," in the sense of a dislike for black men, his indignation would have been amply justified. One does not feel prejudice against a beast of burden: one keeps him between the shafts. General Hertzog, doubtless, believes that there is room for the native there—in the unskilled labour market, whether there is room for him on the land or not—and we have seen the reflection of that belief in those labour provisions of his Land Bill which I have recited.

Whether the Dutch Reformed Church in South Africa agrees or disagrees with the rest of the Christian world on this question of the colour bar, or whether all other Christian communities in South Africa have always themselves been consistent in their practice or precepts with regard to the relations between white and native Christians in Church and State, this is not the place to discuss. But an abandonment of the

doctrine of equal human rights and of the principle that the native is entitled to make use of all
the advantages that education can give him, which
the Christian evangelical missionaries have always
preached as one of the essential treasures of
European civilisation, must infallibly have a
disastrous reaction on the credit and influence of
Christianity among all coloured peoples. The
denominations whose representatives signed the
memorial, and their fellow-members of those
communions in Europe and America, cannot
possibly and certainly will not associate themselves with such an abandonment, and will
doubtless continue protestants against the Colour
Bar Law—an attitude which the progressive
industrial effects of its application will certainly
continuously reinforce.

But more serious than the sectional challenge
to the Asiatic world in the anti-Indian proposals,
and the blow at the reputation of the white man's
professed religion, in General Hertzog's official
repudiation of what, since the days of its fight
against slavery, that religion has comprehensively
stood for in the African world, is the significance,
as it is already recognised by the thinkers and
writers of African race in every part of the world,
of the fact that, for the first time in the history
of the British Empire, distinction of race in
a British Dominion is made the basis of dis-
criminating legislation in this outspoken fashion.
Disabilities have, no doubt, before now, been
indirectly imposed or covertly inflicted; rights

and privileges enjoyed by Europeans have been
withheld; but this is the first outspoken declaration by law that the natives are getting too
numerous and too clever—that the white man
"has to fight an unequal fight against them," and
that his hands must be strengthened for the
conflict by tying those of the black.

What strikes the writer even more forcibly
than the shortsightedness and practical folly of
such a policy—(which aspect, like the memorialists, I leave to be dealt with by the educated
good sense of South Africa, already actively
vocal)—is its extraordinary pusillanimity, its
morbid scepticism of the capacity of white men
and the standard of Western civilisation to keep
their heads above water. It claims that the
white man must govern, without in the least
degree apprehending or considering how and
why it is that he is able to govern, and likely
for a long time to remain able to do so. I suppose
the quality of their own Poor Whites has made
South Africans sceptical; and the worthlessness
of their Poor Whites—I do not say their poverty,
for there are poor white men everywhere—is
directly and admittedly the product and result,
as the corresponding "white trash" was in the
Southern States of America, of the maintenance
of that "peculiar institution" of South Africa,
the Kaffir boy, at any criticism of whose status
in their economy South Africans are just as
touchy as used to be their cousins in the New
World. I have explained how it was that this

slave-state mentality in regard to the Kaffir's divinely appointed rôle was carried over the period between the abolition of chattel slavery and the introduction of capitalised industrialism, which has revived and re-envenomed it. Plenty of South Africans are fully alive to the facts of the situation, though the orthodox Nationalist may wax indignant at a hint of it. That is what is wrong with South Africa. She has never grown up: or, rather, the native policy of the whole Union is now dominated by a majority of voters whose apprehension missed the tide of that emancipatory vision which revolutionised Europe a hundred years ago and subsequently transformed even the slave society of America. Her statesmen are positively able to talk without any consciousness of absurdity about being prepared to allow the Natal-Indian controversy to be settled by a conference, provided this can be effected "consistently with the maintenance of Western standards of life," at the moment when they are enacting a Colour Bar Bill (affecting Indians, though not so seriously as their own natives) which is essentially a considered repudiation of Western standards of life. Western civilisation, in so far as it exists and prevails, is not a mere affair of rates of wages or earnings. It has had its serfs and bondsmen, originally of conquered races, and has decided that a healthy society cannot be founded on that class of labour. All that is most vital in Western civilisation is now engaged in the task of eliminating slavery and exploitation from the operations of the capitalist industrial system, crude intromissions of which have in such sinister fashion affected the industrial world of South Africa, associating a Labour Party which ostensibly exists to contend against the modern slave-holding forces with a Conservative Agriculturist Party desirous to maintain and enforce a mediæval social form and theory of the lower orders.

What is it that the South African Europeans who have got cold feet from reading Mr Cousins' Census Report are afraid of? Do they think that if white civilisation is a good thing it is only strong because it has machine guns and aeroplanes? That it has no real human virtue or strength embodied in it which can attract and help to civilise other races? That African races can come into contact with it without its stirring in them profoundly disturbing ferments? Western civilisation has a very ancient pedigree. It derives from India, Egypt, Greece, Rome, the Catholic Church, and free Christianity. Its fundamental instincts of justice and charity are not different from those of the black man. The more elaborate social inheritance whereby the Western world has sought to adapt life to those instincts has much that attracts the black man, as our economic arts attract and interest him, though there is much in our institutions and morals that horrifies him as profoundly as much in his horrifies us. I am a good European, and I believe in the European achievement—in which, of course, the American is a co-operator. I do not say it is better than every other civilisation or shut my eyes to its appalling shortcomings and failures: but I think it is an enormously better thing than any culture Africa, outside of the Mediterranean and Nilotic area, has produced, and that native Africans recognise this, are attracted by it, profit by it, and, under its stimulus, education, and discipline, are advanced in the faculties of humanity.

CHAPTER XV

THE measure described as "The Areas Reservation and Immigration and Registration (Further Provision) Bill," introduced in the South African Union Parliament in the spring of 1926, had for its declared purpose the diminution of the existing population of Indians in South Africa by the exercise of what the Minister introducing it described as "pressure." To speak more distinctly, by means of oppression; namely, by the withdrawal of existing rights and the application of increasing disabilities to a degree which might render life in South Africa intolerable to Indians who had settled and founded families there under the direct encouragement of South African Governments, especially that of Natal, during the last sixty-six years.

There are now about 155,000 persons of Indian birth or descent in the Dominion. Of these about 135,000 are in Natal, 12,000 in the Transvaal Province, 8000 in the Cape, and 600 in the Orange Free State. In the Transvaal, ever since the establishment of self-government under the Union Constitution, special disabilities have been imposed on Indians, in consonance with the Dutch Afrikander colour policy, but in Natal and the Cape they have been under no disability, except that of disfranchisement for Parliamentary purposes, founded on a provision in the Constitution excluding from such franchise natives of any country not at the time possessing elective representative institutions. This disability was not removed from Indians when the new Indian Constitution establishing similar institutions was enacted. Until quite recently Indians in Natal enjoyed, as they do in Cape Colony, the municipal franchise, but this was withdrawn last year. The Government of Natal had twice previously enacted this disfranchisement, but the laws had been disallowed. On its last re-enactment, General Hertzog's Government sanctioned it.

The legislation recently introduced proposes to withdraw from Indians the right of buying or leasing land anywhere in the Union, except within a belt of thirty miles from the Natal coast, and within this belt only inside such areas as may be determined. It also provides that in townships Indians shall only be entitled to buy or lease property or to be licensed for business within certain defined areas, to be set up on the recommendation of the local municipality (in which Indians are now represented). Within the Natal coast-belt Indians will only be permitted to buy or lease property from other Indians already in possession of it. Indians' licences to trade, where already held outside permitted areas, will ostensibly be renewable to their present holders, but they may be withdrawn, and the unconcealed intention of the policy is that they shall be withdrawn.

The Indian population in Natal was founded by the introduction of immigrants by the Government for the sugar plantations, and this immigration was energetically pressed for many years. Recruiting was persistently carried out in India, and its purposes were effected by persuasion and promises of the advantages which Indians would enjoy in a British Colony founded on the basis of a Royal Proclamation decreeing that no disability or limitation of legal rights should be imposed on anyone by reason of colour, race, or religion. In order to maintain the labour supply, the earlier immigrants were encouraged to settle by grants of land. They were not allowed to return to India until five years after the expiry of their first indentures. Concurrently with the importation of labourers for the sugar plantations many free Indians were encouraged to come in as traders for the supply of the needs of their fellow countrymen. Of these traders and their descendants, as well as of those of the plantation coolies, a good many flocked into the South African Republic after the gold discoveries, and in spite of the persecution to which they were exposed, and which was made a special cause of complaint against Kruger's Government and one of the pleas for the South African War, established prosperous businesses there.

The present policy of anti-Indian legislation is partly a manifestation of racial prejudice, partly a reflection of the industrial colour bar and Kaffir-work theory, and partly due to fear of trading competition by Indians. The last can only be regarded as deserving of consideration in the Colony of Natal. The Indian population in Natal is now increasing very slowly, whilst the white population is increasing comparatively fast, thus showing that Indian competition does not depress it.

The great bulk of the Indian population is, in fact, agricultural and does not seriously compete to the detriment of the classes of cultivation carried on by white residents. The strongest outcry comes from the small trading classes. White traders cannot compete, it is said, in selling goods, with Indians. In selling to whom? To whites? If the selling of goods by Indians (cheaply) to whites injures the white community, that community has the remedy in its own hands. Let whites buy only from whites and pay white traders' prices. If any of them are so disloyal to their colour as to prefer not to, why not pass laws to compel them? Theirs is the offence; it is they that should be disciplined. Is it in selling to Indians? It cannot be an injury to the white that imported Indians should trade with imported Indians or their descendants with one another. Such trading cannot possibly place the white (so long as he himself buys from whites) in, at worst, any worse a position than if no Indians had ever come in or all had been— as is deemed desirable—driven out. In fact, as has always been recognised as a reason for admitting Indian traders, Indian trading is of substantial advantage to white employers of agricultural and other Indian labour.

Is it in selling to natives? There, no doubt, is the rub. The native buys from the Indian because the Indian provides what he wants, sells it to him cheap, and treats him civilly. Does the Indian cheat the native? So, notoriously, does the white trader, and at prices at which the native gets, on a balance, less for his money. What the anti-Indian seeks is European monopoly of exploiting the native black as consumer, just as colour bar legislation aims at European monopoly of exploiting him as producer. Keep wages for natives as low and prices as high as possible.

Again, who are using the low-paid work of Indian painters, tailors, building tradesmen, and engineers? Which colour are these employers, who, an anti-Indian advocate tells us,[1] "*naturally buy labour as cheap as they can*"? If they are whites, all they have to do is to employ white workers only and pay white wages, and they will be at least as well off as if there were no Indians or blacks in South Africa.

The equities of the case in regard to Indians and native demand for their handiwork are the same as I have pointed out in regard to shop-keeping. The whole case for disquiet at Indian competition was examined and reported on about six years ago by a special Commission under Mr

[1] Sir T. Watt, in the *Times*.

Justice Lang. This Commission, which was appointed rather in the hope of finding a case for anti-Indian legislation, made an exceedingly perspicuous and fair-minded report from which, reading between the lines, it is abundantly clear that they thought the case for such legislation an exceedingly weak one. Nevertheless, General Smuts' Government was forced, by the clamour of constituents representing the enfranchised interests concerned, to propose legislation somewhat on the lines of the present Bill. That legislation did not reach maturity, and the Bill introduced by General Hertzog's Government was a good deal more drastic.

Whatever may be, from the point of view of South Africans, the justification of a policy of excluding Asiatics from settlement which, so far as immigration is concerned, is now completely established, and not protested against by Indians, or of a desire that the present Indian population should, if possible, be by equitable means reduced, the questions raised by this Bill are far wider. Continued endeavours have been made in South Africa to encroach upon the rights both actually guaranteed to Indians when they entered the country and assured to them by the unquestioned common law and principle repeatedly proclaimed as dominant in the British Empire. The Indian Government has, with more or less success and with some defeats, continuously protested against and resisted encroachments upon these rights. The Imperial Government has supported them, and has on occasion disallowed local laws infringing them. In 1914, Mr Gandhi, by organising passive resistance in the Transvaal, succeeded in bringing the South African Government to a moderately reasonable attitude, and an agreement was entered into by General Smuts which was regarded both by Gandhi and by the Indian Government as a guarantee against further encroachments. Further encroachments are threatened with all the authority of a self-governing Union Parliament, proposing that existing rights should be taken away and disabilities imposed without compensation in order to exercise effectual "pressure." But the case for the South African policy and the extent of its menace to Indians has unquestionably been overstated by each of the respective parties. They are exaggerated by colour prejudice, vociferous small sectional interests, and the imaginative apprehension of injustice to which contact with Europeans has unfortunately tutored, especially during recent years, both the Asiatic and the African mind.

CHAPTER XVI

SOME SOUTH AFRICAN WITNESSES

"To a student of South African questions nothing is more striking than the interpenetration by the natives of every accessible phase of the life of the white community. One asks, 'What is the foundation of agriculture, of mining, of industry generally?' To this question there is but one answer: the Native. It may be added that household servants are chiefly natives, most of the remainder being coloured." [1]

" It is generally accepted as a well-established custom in South Africa that industry must be based upon the employment of low-paid non-European labourers." [2]

"There shall be no equality of black and white in Church or State." [3]

"The Grondwet, which so clearly, concisely, and cynically laid down the relative positions of black and white, disappeared as a defined policy at the close of the war in 1902, but the practice was not greatly changed." [4]

[1] Mr Stephen Mills, C.M.G., Chairman of the S.A. Economic and Wages Commission, 1925.

[2] *Economic and Wages Commission's Report*, Part II.

[3] *Grondwet of the South African Republic and Constitution of the Orange Free State.*

[4] Maurice Evans, C.M.G., *Black and White in South Africa.*

"The wages of white miners on the Rand are higher than in any other part of the world. . . . White wages (throughout South Africa) are high because non-European wages are low."[1]

"Forced to pay a high rate of wages to white workers . . . producers have found this possible only because of the employment of native labour in the lower branches of industry."

"White wages have been paid and are being paid largely at the expense of the native worker."[2]

"It is obvious that the present level of European wages is due to and dependent on the present level of natives' wages."[3]

"These special provisions" (of the Native Labour Regulation Act of 1911 and the Masters and Servants Acts in the different Provinces) "have the social result of dulling the public conscience against interferences with the freedom of the individual, not only for natives, but for whites as well, so that a feeling tends to be established that the manual worker—whatever his colour—belongs to a different species of animal from other human beings. Those provisions also help to maintain the tradition that manual work is degrading for white people. . . . Economically, these Acts operate to prevent natives as a class from bettering their position."[4]

[1] Chief Inspector of Labour, Union of South Africa.
[2] Federated Chamber of Industries.
[3] *Economic and Wages Commission's Report*, Part I.
[4] *Economic Commission's Report*, Part II.

"In no other land under the British flag, except, perhaps, in the Far East, certainly in none of the great self-governing colonies with which we rank ourselves, is the position of the white man *qua* white man so high, his status so impugnable, as in South Africa. Differing in much else, the race instinct binds the whites together to demand recognition as a member of the ruling and inviolable caste, even for the poorest, the most degraded of their race. And this position connotes freedom from all manual and menial toil. Without hesitation the white man demands this freedom, without question the black man accedes and takes up the burden, obeying the race-command of one who may be his personal inferior. It is difficult to convey to one who has never known this distinction the way in which the very atmosphere is charged with it in South Africa. A white oligarchy, every member of the race an aristocrat; a dark proletariat, every member of the race a server; the line of cleavage as clear and deep as the colours. The less able and vigorous of our race thus protected find here an ease, a comfort, and recognition to which their personal worth would never entitle them in a homogeneous white population." [1]

"The rates of pay of the industrialised and detribalised natives living in towns are so low that they and their families are inadequately fed, clothed, and housed." [2]

[1] Maurice Evans, *Black and White in S.E. Africa.*
[2] *Economic Commission's Report*, Part II.

" The white man in South Africa is fighting an unequal fight against the native." [1]

"Europeans in South Africa have a deep, instinctive, and abiding feeling that, if they and their descendants are to remain there they must not give full political and other rights to the blacks.

" No ethical consideration . . . will be allowed to stand in the way. They may be . . . committing a great wrong to a people for whom they are trustees, and they may raise enmities and forces that will all the more surely and quickly destroy themselves; but they do not think so." [2]

"Familiarity with these extraordinary conditions blinds the average colonist to the singularity of the position, and it is accepted as the normal condition of things. True, the Europeans are not satisfied with the practical outcome . . . but few seem to see the singularity of the whole situation." [3]

South Africa is, in short, in the singular situation, in the British commonwealth of Nations, in the community of Christendom, and practically in the whole of the civilised world, of being still a slave state. The position of the wage-working class in other countries, under the capitalist, industrial, and landowning system, is sometimes spoken of as "wage slavery," but that is a

[1] General Hertzog, speaking in the Union Parliament.
[2] Sir Thomas Watt, *Times*, 30th April 1926.
[3] Maurice Evans, *loc. cit.*

metaphorical use of language intended to indicate that the position of a wage-worker under capitalism is in some of its disabilities comparable to that of a slave. Wage-slavery is an economic position assigned to individuals by the action of competition under the capitalist property system. Slavery is a definite social and industrial status historically antecedent to capitalism, originating generally in conquest, piracy, kidnapping, or violence, and sanctioned and attached to its victims by the social conventions and public law of the slave-owning community. This system has been by progressive stages gradually eliminated from most of the world by the dual action of the influences of Christianity and the evolution of the capitalist system of industry. Slavery (as Cairnes, one of the most perspicuous pioneers of modern sociological economics, originally pointed out in his essay, "The Slave Power," on the slave economy of the Southern United States) breaks itself down and secretes intolerable, internal, social poisons wherever it is pressed into the service of commercial production. Capitalism supersedes it, being economically a more efficient productive system. I have pointed out, from the undisputed testimony of authoritative South African witnesses, the fact that when the legal status of slavery was nominally abolished in 1834 the social and economic status remained firmly established, and that the white community in all the territories now forming the Union maintained the spirit and clung to and enforced the theory of a slave society, namely that labour for the conqueror is the proper function of the men of the conquered and expropriated race and a disgrace to the dominant white. That the Boers, who quitted the Cape in protest against the abrogation of the law of slavery, carried that law with them, and maintained its principle in their political constitutions and in their Masters and Servants Laws. I have said, where much might be said, practically nothing at all about the detestable and despicable efflorescence of colour prejudice by which the baser elements of the character of the North European races that have colonised South Africa manifest themselves in the action, language and behaviour towards natives and Indians not only of low-class whites in all the Provinces, but even of conspicuous politicians. These arrogancies and insolences and repudiations of human decencies and dignities, in contrast to which the habitual behaviour not only of most other European peoples, but of Africans and Indians themselves, puts to shame the brutish manners quite common and conspicuous among South Africans—are the natural and familiar products in uncivilised, domineering and mean-spirited temperaments of the position of self-imputed superiority which every white lout assumes in a slave society as his birthright. These fashions of asserting and demonstrating the dignity of their race are for the reputable and civilised Europeans part of the white man's burden in Africa. But the civilised minority sometimes appear strangely acquiescent in and tolerant of the discredit which their exhibition earns for the South African white man. Mr Gandhi, assuredly, has contributed something towards South African white education in human behaviour and sensibility, and his successors in the campaign for the vindication of Indians' rights have continued the process. Indians have also been able to bring to bear in their support the advocacy of governments standing upon the principles of free civilisation both in India and in this country. The native has, in the political world, no such organised backing. His spokesmen can only appeal as they do to the more enlightened minority of South Africans and to the community of the Christian Churches. Colour prejudice, in its more contemptible aspects, the misbehaviour and injustice of many Europeans to natives, the ravings of such mental defectives as Mr Tielman Roos, are merely the familiar characteristic reactions of the social and economic atmosphere of the slave state, and can only be effectively altered through the modification of its spirit and working methods.

The reason why I say little on the phenomenon of "colour prejudice," in the sense in which I have just referred to it, is because in these viler and more degrading manifestations it is a symptom rather than an originating cause. It is a secondary product of repressive institutions and social conventions which have arisen not out of an initial aversion to coloured races, but out of an undisciplined interest in taking advantage of their weakness and ignorance to use them for the white man's profit, and of the reactions of such institutions and oppressions in breeding contempt and fear in inferior minds. The slave relation, being once established, is automatically and in part unconsciously buttressed by a resolute refusal to admit that the slave is capable of anything better; and when, in the development of competitive industrialism, opportunities arise for his showing that he is capable, the fear of his competition with the established master race adds feelings of jealousy and hatred to the fear and contempt, and reinforces the obstinacy of the refusal to admit any kind of equality of capacity or of rights. His education and his free use of his faculties are discouraged and opposed. In low minds this complex of prejudices and resistances breeds open contumely, vilification of the slave-race, agitation against any concessions to it, and acts of outrage and violence.

Moreover, it is not in the form of colour prejudice of this virulent type that preconceptions against an intelligent native policy are really a prevailing or principal cause of repressionism in South Africa. I have referred to the singular disturbance of spirit exhibited by General Hertzog in the debate on the Colour Bar Bill, at the imputation which he conceived had been made against his policy that it was actuated by colour prejudice, whereas it was quite simply intended merely to strengthen the white man in his position of economic privilege. A psycho-analyst—one of the sort that sticks at nothing—would indeed without hesitation attribute such a hysterical and unprovoked tirade as that which I quoted to some deep-seated racial *libido* or inherited fear, such as quite commonly manifests itself in the dealings of Boers with natives. The tradition of Dingaan's massacre, and other sufferings of the Boers while at war, without quarter, against the natives —their own retaliatory atrocities, in starving Zoutpansberg Kaffirs to death, blockaded on krantzes and in caves, not only are remembered and often referred to, but have unquestionably implanted in many of the Boer stock that "deep-seated, instinctive, and abiding conviction" as to how to deal with natives, which manifested itself in the otherwise quite inexplicable proceedings of the Administrator of mandated South-West Africa, and of the volunteers who eagerly assembled to help him under "the blessing of God" in destroying with machine guns and aeroplanes half the miserable remnant of the Bondelswaart Hottentot tribe on the pretext of "rebellion." Not that they had rebelled;—but because they were suspected of an intention to resist the arrest of Abraham Morris, who had been Botha's chief native scout in the war against the Germans, and who had returned to his native land without the formality of a permit. About that episode, when it was "inquisitorially" canvassed by the Mandates Commission of the League of Nations, the Union Government evidently, and very discreetly, thought that the less said the better. Their Administrator's face had to be saved, as the white man's face always has to be in any South African dealings with natives.

But deep-seated as is this fear-complex, with its associated cruelty complex, among South Africans, and sinister as are its occasional explosions in action and language, or ludicrous as is General Hertzog's nightmare-outcry that the white man in South Africa is fighting an unequal fight against the native, it is probably not the strongest support of obscurantism and stupidity in questions of native policy. Colour prejudice, of that really vile kind to which I have cursorily alluded, is not characteristic of the typical farming South African, whether of Boer or other stock. It is, for reasons I have explained, more fundamentally characteristic of city and industrial outlanders. The real strength of the Nationalist policy in regard to native relations (temporarily in alliance with the militant economic self-interest of the South African Labour Party) lies in a system of deep-seated, partly benevolent and quite arguable convictions about the native, combined with economic self-interest, the character of which is very clearly indicated in the reflections published in Mr D. C. De Waal's account of his journey *With Rhodes in Mashonaland* in 1890 and 1891. Mr De Waal, then M.L.A. of the Cape Colony, appears in this book as a man of sympathetic and engaging personality, a fine South African type, and must have been a first-rate companion to travel with. He is full of big-heartedness and capability, mixed with small pawkinesses and cautiousnesses. He has some of the characteristics of Boswell as a biographer: shrewd impressionability, extreme naïveté, great self-conceit, and an entire freedom from inhibitions of judgment about the Englishmen with whom he came in contact, especially Lord Randolph Churchill and British Army officers, whose measure he and his fellow racials had got pretty accurately at the outbreak of the Boer War. He admired Rhodes, and had Rhodes been as interesting a character as was Dr Johnson, or had Mr De Waal not generally been conscious of himself as much more interesting than Rhodes (which, as a character, to an Englishman, who knows all about Rhodes, he really is) he might have written a great biography. As it is, his observations are most revealing of the South African farmers' attitude.

He describes an interview between Sir H. Loch, the High Commissioner, and Mankoroaan, the Bechuana Chief at Taungs. Mankoroaan had complained of the boundary set up between British Bechuanaland and the Transvaal, which had cut his tribe's lands in two. The British Government had, in fact, after sending up Sir Charles Warren to head off certain Transvaal "filibusters" who were breaking westwards, merely drawn their boundary line just as far east as was wanted for the route of Rhodes's Cape to Cairo telegraph line and railway, taking Mankoroaan under their sovereignty, but leaving part of his tribe outside. Sir Henry Loch thought Mankoroaan unreasonable and indeed ungrateful, more especially as Mankoroaan bluntly told him that his people would have been better off if the whole of his country had been left inside the Transvaal boundary. Rhodes and Mr De Waal discussed the matter afterwards.

"Our Premier," says Mr De Waal, "was of opinion that the sooner the people of Mankoroaan were compelled to work for the farmers, the sooner they would learn to their advantage that it was the duty of every man, be he black or white, to earn his bread by toil—and shepherds or labourers were just then what farmers were most in need of. I, too, felt—and Mr Venter shared the feeling with me—that there existed far too much ungratefulness and impoliteness in Mankoroaan and his men towards their benefactors. They should be forced to do labour under the farmers. The sooner Bechuanaland is annexed to the Cape the better, not only for those lazy lords personally, and the country in which they live, but for the general civilisation and prosperity of the land." British Bechuanaland was soon afterwards transferred from Government by the Crown to that of the Cape Colony.

On his return journey, Mr De Waal met a party of natives who were on the way to the goldfields. "It was a pretty sight," he says, "to see them march—all in faultless step and everyone dressed in white cloth. They were young, tall, strong Matabele, with beautifully shaped bodies. As we passed them each one politely saluted us. Again I thought, 'What excellent labourers these men would make for the white man!' If Kaffirs only knew the advantages of serving under white masters, they would gain more civilisation in one year than they do from missionaries in fifty; selling wives as slaves would cease, polygamy would die out, and they would have a fair opportunity of hearing the Word of God, for wherever the white man is, there also are churches [1] and preachers. As it is, there is now a general scarcity of labourers: Kaffirs can live so easily that they decline to be dependent (*sic*) on the European. They are, however, beginning to recognise their degraded position, and some of them already know the privileges to be enjoyed by being servants to the white man. We may hope that the day will soon dawn when not a single farmer will need to complain of being short of labour.[2] When that time comes the productions of our land will become double what they are at present, even though its population should not increase, and there will be general content and progress." With this perfectly straightforward and convinced presentation (enunciated not controversially but as a private enunciation of obvious truths) of the

[1] To which natives are not admitted.

[2] Rhodes, on this journey having promised one old pioneer farmer that Matabeleland would be annexed at the first opportunity.

Nationalist farmers' view, I will collate Maurice Evans's testimony.

"The demand for absolute submission by the Dutch farmer sometimes resulted in forcing it by extreme cruelty (cases sometimes come up before the Courts which make one throb with indignation), but the normal position was that he took an interest in the lives and affairs of his dependents and often made their simple lives comfortable to them to an extent that was rare in the landowners of the other white races. I have often been struck at meetings of large numbers of Dutch families on occasions such as Nachtmaals, when the tent wagons were outspanned on the Kerkplein, with the apparently pleasant and accepted relations between the members of the family and the black servants. The latter, especially the girls, are nearly always neatly and suitably dressed, are often well trained, and have a look of docile confidence and well-doing that denotes content and is pleasant to witness. Not nearly so often does one see these same relations around the homestead of the British farmer. There is more 'drive,' modern conditions come into operation, and though business fairplay may be granted to the native which would not be understood by the Dutchman, and though extreme severity would not be meted out on occasion, I feel that the patriarchal condition, with all its limitations, is better understood and more appreciated by the native."

So also did West Indian and Southern planters

argue the merits of slavery. But Maurice Evans does not argue for the patriarchal system; he advocates the freeing of the natives to his own life, under disinterested white guidance, in his own communities. The patriarchalism, if any, to be official.

Witness is also borne in the Report of the Economic Commission to the fact that within the framework of the presumptions of their patriarchal society, the theory of di inely appointed authority of white over black, and of permanent distinction of status, the Boers have understood well how to deal with the native, and have enjoyed his confidence. This recognition does not, however, affect the Commission's conviction that the theory of that system cannot be defended, being rooted in fallacious habits of mind implanted by and directly derived from slavery, and because it has not only resulted in producing the "poor white" class, but now, in association with the development of industrial economic relations introduced by the capitalist system of wage employment, is setting up disastrous antagonisms between black and white in the wage-labour market. These latter-day developments, in fact, are bringing out the inherent poisons of the theory of native status and "Kaffir work" which supports the whole South African social structure, as writing in invisible ink will be brought out by the touch of fire or acid. That is why that Eirenicon to the native which General Hertzog propounds as a Native Land

Bill, and which, in fact, boils down to nothing more than a scheme for establishing all the natives outside the Reserves in the position so piously desired for them by Mr De Waal, that of bound labourers for South African farmers, really appears to many, probably to most, of General Hertzog's constituents as a genuinely philanthropic and statesmanlike measure, which will be so beneficial and civilising to the native that he will recognise the blessings of that position, and his increasing numbers will no longer appear a menace to white supremacy.

The natives do not see it in that light. The Economic Commission are under no such illusion. Nor, so far as I have been able to discover, does any South African publicist of any estimation in that country as intelligent or authoritative uphold it as a conceivably stable or workable policy. Mr De Waal is a comparatively enlightened exponent of it, and the positive limitations of Mr De Waal's intelligence and of his faculties of sympathy and imagination are piquantly conspicuous on every page of his book. . . . Mr De Waal dreams of contented Kaffirs earning their bread by toil in smiling farm homesteads. He records some impressive examples of the "proper relations" between masters and servants. He had, on one occasion, "anything but a kind feeling towards the Premier, who had no business whatever to interfere with the inspanning," but who beat Mr De Waal's boy, whose business it was, "for imaginary laziness," and got him half-

killed by a mule-kick. He also thought Mr
Lange, another of his companions, "unreasonable" for giving (after a convivial supper) another
servant "a severe thrashing—a punishment wholly
undeserved." But when his own portmanteau
had got torn by a tree on the march and his pipe
and some underclothing had dropped from it,
and with them a palm nut he had carried several
thousand miles to show (kindly man) to his
children ("that I would not have sold for ten
pounds"), "I felt so sad and out of humour
about it that I abandoned my intention of going
on with the rest of the party, and resolved to set
out instead in search of my palm-nut. But the
rest of the party would not hear of my turning
back, . . . so it was at last decided that Roeping
and January should return in the wagon's track
and find the missing things, *failing to do which
we promised to give them each twenty-four
lashes.*" The fateful nut was retrieved, having
doubtless commanded the reverence of way-
farers, who, however, had been overcome by the
coarser appeal of the pipes and the pantaloons,
for these had vanished. In the rejoicing over the
nut the promised penalty was remitted. One
doubts, however, whether, if it had not been, the
Kaffirs could have justly discriminated between the
different disciplinary principles pursued by Mr
Rhodes, Mr Lange, and Mr De Waal respectively.
Mr De Waal may not have intended to carry
out his threat; but the fact that it could be
plausibly made, and regarded by both parties as

a quite admissible incident is sufficiently significant. Mr De Waal admired those young Matabele braves. Did he, one wonders, reflect what they would look like as detribalised Kaffir boys cadging for jobs in white men's cast-off slop clothing or taking a flogging for losing a palm-nut? No race can be raised by destroying its self-respect. That is the cruellest and most deadly thing that white men's civilisation can do to natives.

CHAPTER XVII

THE CONVERSION OF KENYA

THE case of Kenya, to which I have referred in Chapter VII, is so significant in connection with this Anatomy that it is worth returning to. Any middle-aged Englishman accustomed to take for granted the traditions of British Colonial rule, but who had not had time or occasion to follow in detail the evolutionary biology of latter-day Imperial development in Africa, must repeatedly have felt puzzled about the attitude displayed in Kenya by white men, reputed to be English settlers, and in a modified degree by the local Government, supposed to be directed by the British Colonial Office, in the recurrent controversies about the respective rights and duties of Europeans and natives which have from time to time developed sufficient tension to claim notice in the British Press and Parliament.

It has puzzled him that whereas the Duke of Devonshire informed the Kenya Government in his Memorandum of July 1923 that "His Majesty's Government record their considered opinion that the interests of the African natives must be paramount, and that if and when those interests and those of the immigrant races should conflict, the former should prevail," Lord Cranworth, speaking at the Royal Colonial Institute

178

in April 1926, should pronounce that "Never must the interests of the white population be allowed to be swamped by the interests of the natives."

Still more disconcerting has it been to him—believing and thanking God that his Empire was a bringer of liberty and welfare to Africans, and remembering that East Africa was gathered within its fold by treaties with her tribal chiefs as a Protectorate for the natives, and subsequently made a "Crown" Colony as a token and assurance to them that they should be governed in accordance with the principles which had caused the name of the Great Queen and her House to be revered throughout Africa as a guarantee of freedom and justice—to read of prominent settlers arguing before a Native Commission against the allowance of adequate land reserves to the natives on the ground, most tersely put by Lord Delamere, that "If the policy was to be continued, that every native was to be a landholder of a sufficient area on which to establish himself, then the question of obtaining a sufficient labour-supply would never be settled."

This was not intended to mean that if the natives all had land they would not have enough labour to work it with: it meant that there would not be enough want among natives to cause them to supply sufficient labour for whites.

Why, asks our Englishman—on the principles of the Devonshire Memorandum—should there be? Why should not white immigrants do their

own work, as Mr Atherston advised they should
in Southern Rhodesia, or employ white men?
And why does "labour," in these discussions,
always seem to mean only the employment of
blacks by whites and not natives' own industry,
and an African "labour shortage" or "famine"
or "problem" always mean some entirely imported
and gratuitous affliction of white men at not
getting enough of something which there is no
obvious justification for their thinking they have
a right to expect to get at all?

Still more disconcerted was such a simple
person when—after a large importation of Englishmen who had fought to make the world safe
for democracy and to release Africa from those
Hunnish oppressions which were so movingly
described in the British Government's War Blue
Book on German Colonies, with a special stress
on forced labour—the Government of Kenya
not only put official duress on chiefs to find
labour for planters, but passed an ordinance to
compel such labour by force of law, and when
Lord Milner defended the principle in the House
of Lords on the ground that such discipline would
educate the native to love work and revere its
dignity. When Lord Milner's successor, Mr
Churchill, following in this field of policy the
line he had always taken in regard to native
rights, sat firmly down on the ordinance and
nothing more was heard for some time of forced
labour, our Englishman supposed he had had a
bad dream and that Dr Norman Leys was a liar,

an impression in which he has been quite recently confirmed by Sir Edward Grigg's describing it as a "truism" that "the Government neither can nor will produce labour from the reserves by compulsion of any sort—and it is therefore idle to call upon the Government to guarantee a supply of labour sufficient to meet all demands, present and future, of private enterprise." The Governor has a nice touch. "Truism," says he! One wonders what Lord Milner's ghost thought of that. That is just what the silly Englishman had always thought it was. How was it that he had that bad dream? Sir Edward Grigg expressed sympathy with the desperation and impatience of the white farmers. Why are they desperate, and why deserving of sympathy?

Because from the first in Kenya the establishment of European settlement has been forced in a blindly reckless manner. The local and Imperial authorities responsible, whether the latter were the Foreign Office or the Colonial Office, have certainly been actuated by high Imperial purposes and, according to their lights, by theoretically philanthropic intentions towards the natives—although their views as to what is good for native have been, to say the least of it, both debatable and, in their formulations, erratic. Fortunately their variation has tended in the direction of intelligence and sanity. Both Downing Street and the local administration now really seem to be learning their job and to be steadying themselves on lines of policy much less

disastrous than those which were being followed
up to a few years ago. For now Mr Ormsby
Gore repudiates Lord Delamere and Lord Milner,
and says that if native Africans are allowed and
encouraged to develop their own cultivation upon
their own land they will furnish an increasing and
improving supply of wage labourers for white
planters and foreigners.

I need not further touch on the question of
native land rights. That battle has, one may hope,
been won, and the Government is now expressly
committed with the maintenance of defensible
principles. There was plenty of land available
for Europeans to colonise without depriving the
natives of land they were occupying or needed;
and Europeans had an incontestable right to plant
themselves on such vacant lands, as they did on
those of Australia and New Zealand. I leave
out of account certain acts of injustice that have
been perpetrated in the process of dividing the
land between Europeans and the natives and any
question of the adequacy of the reserves assigned
for the natives' use. But we have recognised the
fruit of the example of Mr Rhodes' and Mr De
Waal's methods of treating their native servants
in the deaths of Kenya servants from flogging or
"tying up" for equally trivial or imaginary
offences, and the refusal of white juries to convict
the offenders of anything more than inflicting
"grievous bodily harm"—a form of verdict
bearing valiant witness to the indestructibility of
the soul and to the negligible achievement of

those who merely kill the body. When attention was called in England to these scandals there was indignant protest against their being regarded as justification for imputations against the temper of the white settlers. They were, we were assured, quite foreign to the spirit of Britons, and were no doubt regarded with horror by the community. That is partially true: partially still untrue. In so far as Kenya has absorbed the South African inheritance of the slave theory of the natives' natural functions, such outrages have not been condemned locally, and the condemnation of them is still resented. Englishmen in Kenya have got to exorcise that South African theory, and it may be hoped are in process of doing so.

All the land available for European settlement has now been appropriated, either in freehold or on leases for 999 years. Settlement has been encouraged and pushed with insufficient regard to the possibilities of the lands disposed of being brought into such a degree of agricultural use as to yield to the class of settlers who have been encouraged to go out a livelihood on the standard they have been led to expect. Much of this over-forcing of settlement has been done and is still being done through the agency of land syndicates or holders for sale. The theory of this kind of capitalist colonisation is perfectly simple. Emigrants are sent out for the establishment of the Empire and for the profit of the grantees of the land. A few of those who go from England are working farmers or labourers: they are buoyed on the established assumption of the average young man of the middle and upper classes of our society that all that a man of those classes needs in order to make a living in a new colony is to get hold of suitable land and to employ "labour." The seventeenth century companies who promoted colonisation in America and at the Cape quickly recognised that "labour" did not automatically, in an uncivilised country not endowed with a floating reserve of a million unemployed wage-seekers, supply itself. They spiritedly kidnapped negroes and furnished the planters with slaves. The earlier settlers in Kenya, not being English public schoolboys or demobilised soldiers, but principally farmers from South Africa and Rhodesia, were under no illusion that "labour" would appear at their invitation to produce paying crops demanding high cultivation under their enlightened direction and kindly patronage. Neither their Government nor the Development Syndicate that introduced them could supply them with Malay or West Coast slaves: but they, unlike the early Cape and American settlers, were in a position to put effective pressure upon the natives. Their Government had irresistible powers and knew how to use them. So they frankly demanded that the Government should restrict the reserves and, when that pressure failed, compel the native to work by law. That theory of colonial development is the modern Imperial mongrel offspring of slavedom and capitalist Imperialism. It came into Kenya out

184

of the womb of the modern slave state of the South African Union, the peculiar institutions of which—the Kaffir boy and the colour bar, and their morbific reactions—I have analysed, and which has just produced that promising new litter of Bills for a Native Policy.

Meanwhile the white settlers, inveigled many of them into a disastrous situation, are deserving of sympathy. There is no question of the difficulties of their position. The development of much more than one-fifth of the alienated land by the existing population is an impossibility. The Report of a recent local Labour Commission makes it baldly clear that more coffee alone had been planted than can be harvested even if the whole available native labour force could be turned out to deal with it. Just as South African economy has been prejudiced by the over-capitalisation of the mines, so has the economy of colonisation in Kenya been prejudiced and jeopardised by the too-rapid forcing of settlement. The Governor has refused to concede the demands for forced labour. But he admitted that the Government of Kenya carries a special responsibility in regard to labour, not borne by Governments in Europe—doubtless meaning that the Kenya Government in the past had invited Colonists to settle and sold them land under a dispensation in which the slave state theory and policy had the upper hand in Government councils, and showed promise of permanently establishing its acceptance.

The situation in Kenya, as regards the demands that are made upon the native, the pressure that is put upon him, and the labour hunger of the white settlers, has been aggravated not only by the excessive forcing of settlement, but also by the excessive demand for the development of the white men's lands by railway construction. Just as the mines force into South Africa an over-capitalised block of exploiting activity, so the demand of the white men that railways shall be made to their lands has forced an over-capitalised block of exploiting activity into Kenya. And after the Colonial Office have abandoned the support of the policy of the direct forcing of labour for private profit, it adhered to the policy of forcing labour for the indirect profit of the white settlers by permitting the Government to impress labour for railways, on the pretext that they were works of public utility. This feverish process, intended, as it was, to relieve the desperate position of the white settlers in regard to shipping their produce, has aggravated their position in another direction by competing with their labour supply.

Sir Edward Grigg handles, as well he may, this aspect of the Government's responsibility very delicately. He gives the best advice possible under the circumstances, that settlers should abandon coffee, sisal, tea, and similar crops requiring much labour, and take to ranching and corn-growing. But what a prospect for the unfortunate settlers who have been tempted by the glowing accounts of the profits to be made

186

from intensive planting to buy land from the middlemen to whom the Government sold it with a view to rapid settlement! There has been, we read, considerable criticism of that part of the Governor's speech, and the Convention to which it was addressed urged the grant of a further measure of self-government to Kenya. Our simple-minded Englishmen may possibly not surmise any connection between these two expressions of view. If he does, he may feel some suspicion whether the complete conversion of Kenya can be regarded as guaranteed.

To a student of the psychology of Imperial expansionism Kenya Colony offers a clinical subject of peculiar interest. There are two motives which bring the white man into contact with coloured races. White men go to uncivilised lands to make money or a livelihood, desiring to benefit themselves: and they go also as missionaries, desiring to benefit the natives. From the time of the Spanish colonisation (which purported to combine the two purposes—the benefit to the white being economic, to the native, religious) until the period of the Partition of Africa very few people imagined or pretended that the two purposes were harmonious: in fact both parties—the colonisers and the missionaries —generally thought the contrary and were continually at issue with each other. Then emerged the brilliant idea that colonisation was The White Man's Burden, and that those who extended the Empire were serving both Mammon and God.

The British Public took kindly to this belief: its sentiments towards coloured and native peoples being fundamentally decent. Lord Balfour and other high-minded Englishmen, during the War and during the Peace negotiations, made great running with the doctrine that English Colonial Government was a Providence to the natives and that German colonies had better be handed over to her to govern. President Wilson and the Allies jumped at the notion and invented the dogma of trusteeship. But this was really a little hard on the men of the old-fashioned school of colonists who were simply out to make their own living as settlers or to make money as company-floaters out of other white men who might attempt to do so. East Africa and Uganda were not, in fact, annexed for the sake of the natives: but to get cotton and trade. Kenya Colony was merely a by-product of the Uganda Railway. Sir Charles Eliot thought it would make a good white man's country. The missionaries co-operated, not at all with the same idea as that which encouraged the settlers. The Protectorate Government started off with unrestricted forced labour for "public" purposes: the leading settlers fought against a fair land policy for the natives: Sir Percy Girouard clapped on heavy taxation to make the natives work. All the time these unfortunate settlers, with their simple primeval colonising mentality—identical with that of their Anglo-Saxon forefathers—feeling no question of their right to take the natives' land or to exploit

his labour, have had to contend with these latter-
day notions which seem to them merely the old
missionary nonsense in a new dress—reinforced
with all the prestige of an international doctrine
of Trusteeship. They cannot understand or
endure it. Even about Tanganyika they write
furiously to the *Times* complaining that Germans
(in a mandated territory) are given equal privileges
with Englishmen, and natives allowed to grow
coffee.

Sir Robert Coryndon (one of Jameson's Matabeleland "looters") was rather astutely chosen
by the Colonial Office as a Governor whose ante-
cedents might give them confidence. He pro-
mulgated what is called the "Dual Policy"—as to
which I have quoted Mr Ormsby Gore (at p. 80).
If that policy is honestly worked it may meet
the necessities of the case: but notwithstanding
the pronouncements of Governor and Under-
Secretaries there are continual edgings away from
it, and the demand for "self government"—
viz. the government of two and a half million
natives by eighteen hundred white landowners—is
primarily aimed at upsetting it. Even Governors
and Secretaries of State still talk resoundingly
about the blessings of civilisation to the natives:
meaning capitalist employment—which is *not* the
best we can do for him. They still talk as if they
believed that men can be made industrious by
being compelled to work—and to work for other
men's profit—ignoring the lessons of our earlier
colonial experience, and the fact that industrial

energy was entirely destroyed throughout the
East Indies by the compulsion to work for others
—and is only being revived by the policy of help-
ing them to work for themselves—as they do in
West Africa, and as the Jamaica peasantry are
learning to do through their 250 local Agricultural Societies. Meanwhile, as I have said, these
secular-minded settlers, who did not go into this
business as a "sacred trust" for the natives, but
with very much the same notions about what
is good for them as those entertained by Mr
Rhodes and Mr De Waal, are deserving of a
certain amount of sympathy in their somewhat
disappointing position. But that position certainly cannot be mended by any concessions
towards a return to the lines of policy which
they used so truculently to seek to impose on
some of their earlier Governors.

African races know better than any others in
the world what slavery and compulsion are.
They are not in the least degree deceived by any
camouflaging of them in the guise of education
for their own benefit. On the contrary, they are
excessively suspicious, and, out of an excess of
caution and of generations of bitter experience,
often give white men less credit than they really
deserve for good will and good faith towards them,
and for offering them opportunities that would
really be to their advantage—even from their own
point of view, as white settlement in Kenya
may assuredly do.

CHAPTER XVIII

IT is amazing, to anyone familiar with parts of the world in which the capacities of Africans have had a chance of technical and agricultural training, to find, from the serious discussion devoted to the question of the existence of such capacities in the Economic Commission's Report, that there appears to be still prevalent in South Africa a theory that the negroid races are incapable of the productive arts of Western civilisation. One would imagine that no notice had ever been taken of the progress of the negro in America, where Bryce said he had learnt as much in two generations as the Anglo-Saxon did in 600 years: or in communities such as the British West Indies, where similar advance is unquestionable and unquestioned. The daily life of such communities proves that if the black man had education and opportunities he is capable both of learning the trades and acquiring the more valuable elements of Western civilisation, though capitalist industrialism will never be congenial to him. He is too human for that. The Bantu is at least as good material as the West African negro stocks, from which the American and West Indian black man came. South African writers constantly say he is better. There may be comparatively few fully educated and civilised South African natives: but there are enough as a sample. The majority of such natives are without elementary white education: they cannot even talk English. "Kitchen Kaffir" is largely the *lingua franca* of the Cape and Natal, and the natives are not encouraged to speak English in preference. The Boers have done better for them by making them learn the Taal. Of course the African generally has not the social heritage of the European. Equally obviously, the average tribal African native is less well-prepared to be amenable to the arts and economic methods of European civilisation than is the average transplanted African racial of America and the West Indies who has been employed, educated, and Christianised for several generations in close association with societies of European culture. In South Africa the native has been deliberately and as fully as possible excluded from the training of such contact, and only those "contemptible people," the missionaries, have attempted to help him to adapt himself or believed in the possibility of his doing so. But that the capacity is not excluded in his racial endowment of human potentialities is abundantly manifest. There are already in America, the West Indies, West Africa, and even South Africa, so many adult black men well above the average of European capacity, in both intellectual professions and manual trades, that it is astonishing to find the Economic Commission carefully taking evidence, or opinion, upon such questions as whether the African's mental capacities are not arrested at puberty. In South Africa, very possibly, so far as some capacities required for white civilisation are concerned, they often are; and the average, and under present social conditions the majority, are, and under those conditions are likely to remain, unsuited for the demands of European industrial civilisation or political institutions. No doubt the exceptions appear exceptional; but their mere existence knocks the bottom out of the argument for a colour bar. And, in fact, the colour bar agitation as a practical force is actuated not by the theory that the native is irremediably incapable of European civilisation, but by the disquieting recognition that he is only too capable of it, and that the trouble about him is, not that he cannot learn, but that he can and does learn, but is able to live on a lower rate of pay for what he can do as well as the European. But that is not his fault. He can only get low pay. The remedy for any danger to white workers from this sort of competition is perfectly well understood by every intelligent student of economics. The South African Labour Party, unless they have really adopted the economic theories of the most benighted of our industrial politicians in this country, and hold that industrial difficulties can be solved only by cutting down wages, must understand it perfectly well. The Economic Commission understood it perfectly well, and repeat it again and again in varying phrases. For example:

"The public regulation of wages should be first applied to those occupations in which the lowest rates are being paid. . . . The effect of such a policy will be, first, to lessen the gap between skilled rates and unskilled rates in industry generally, and so to soften the fall to those European workers whom industry is unable to employ at the present skilled rate. . . . It will improve the chances of the European being employed in preference to the native by eliminating the possibility of paying the native at less than the true market value of his labour. . . . It is only if the native's rate, after all due allowance is made for his lower efficiency, still makes his labour cheaper than the European's, that the native will be preferred."

"Any application of legal wage regulation should be made district by district; it should take existing rates as its starting-point and basis, and it should deal first with the lowest-paid class of labour, irrespective of colour. The best hope for the poorer white workers is the establishment of a standard of pay for unskilled labour which will encourage a reorganisation of industry on the basis of utilising all labour to its maximum capacity, without depriving of employment any of the workers now employed. The position of the white man as an unskilled worker is depressed by a low-wage labour policy; the economic position of the native must be raised or the unskilled white man must go down to the native's standard of living. As industry increases and new industries

such as platinum mining arise, there will be strong
pressure to provide the necessary number of low-
paid non-European workers to allow of these
industries being extended on a low-wage labour
basis.   As long as the gold industry is allowed to
import such labour from outside the Union, the
precedent exists which will make it very difficult
to resist that process; and so long as that importation continues, so long will the opportunities
for employment of workers with a civilised
standard of living be restricted.

"The price paid by South Africa for its native
labour policy is the existence of large numbers of
'poor whites' for whom employment cannot be
found, whilst it is necessary to import a certain
number of men from abroad for skilled posts" (because there is no opening for South African whites
to learn their trade by entering its lowest ranks,
there affording only Kaffir work).

"Natives to-day are mainly employed on
machines, except in so far as they are engaged on
the rough labouring work at which they are little
inferior to white men: they are paid by results
and much more adequately supervised."

The Colour Bar Law, which purports to enact
the prohibition of natives from being employed
on machines, does not really contemplate that.
It contemplates the restriction of contracts and
supervisory jobs to white men, who are to be paid
for the work turned out by the natives who handle
the drills, etc., but who are to be classed and paid
as unskilled labourers.

Amazing, too, it is to anyone who has devoted much study to the relations between white and coloured races in the process of colonisation, both in various parts of Africa and in the New World, and has experienced even a moderate degree of contact with the resulting social conditions, and with people of the African stocks, to observe, in reviewing the South African scene, the naïve presumption, or, shall I say, self-satisfied complacency of the attitude maintained towards the native by the dominant European and by the white skilled labour class, and their apparent confidence that the native must and will accept it contentedly.

Mr Maurice Evans, in the wise and very admirable book I have already quoted, has noted the peculiar purblind mentality, in this aspect, of his fellow colonists in Natal—a mentality, of course, largely unconscious—and discusses its characteristics and causes. His comments are expressed in very moderate and unprovocative language, but they are exceedingly penetrating, and, in effect, profoundly caustic. I will quote just a few of the things I would rather he said for me: I might be suspected of slandering my high-minded and liberty-loving fellow racials.

"A people under democratic conditions have in South Africa the task of governing a very much larger population living in the midst of them, who have no word in such government.

196

"While the natives are quiet, labour is plentiful, and the white man is prospering and making money, the usual course is to ignore them, and only pass such legislation affecting them as will tend to quietude and in cases help and not hinder their exploitation." (Oh, fie! Mr Evans! that sort of talk is what, to-day, we call Bolshevism.) "The common attitude of electors and representatives alike is indifference to the native question; and yet this electorate, for the most part unlearned in all affecting the natives, and usually so busy about its own affairs as to be culpably careless about them and their interests, has in its hands all ultimate power—a power which may easily become very dangerous. In the Transvaal . . . the Grondwet, which so clearly, concisely, and cynically laid down the relative positions of black and white, disappeared as a defined policy at the close of the war in 1902, but the practice was not greatly changed. State and municipal regulations were based on the superiority of the white man, and the position of the races was that of employer and employed. I need not recite the privileges given to the one race and the disabilities placed on the other; if quoted in detail, they would fully justify the general conclusions laid down. The keynote was the absolute governance of the white man. . . ."

"From a practical experience of nearly thirteen years in the Natal Legislature, I know how little the just claims and the interests of the unrepresented receive attention at the hands of Parliament. . . . Too often the pressure of a score of influential constituents and voters will weigh down, with a representative, the known wants of the inarticulate and unrepresented."

Mr Evans wrote thus of the causes of the Zulu rebellion of 1906:

"Since Natal took over responsible government in 1893 no less than forty-eight new laws specially applicable to the native population were passed, and many new regulations framed under these and previous laws. These laws and regulations pressed upon the daily life of the native on all sides, they imposed conditions and restrictions with which he had to comply before he could travel in the country, they put special disabilities upon him in respect of crime—cattle-stealing, to wit; they increased the taxes he had to pay, they interfered with his social life. And, though every year saw new edicts passed which he was bound to obey, there was no provision by which the uneducated native could be told and made to clearly understand the obligations which a legislature—in which he was not represented—imposed upon him. In his ignorance he broke the law of which he had never heard, the police arrested him, and he was fined or imprisoned. I know a case in which new regulations were issued by Government in a *Gazette*, which reached a certain small country town at 9 a.m. The European police opened it, read the regulations, and saw a native just outside infringing them and arrested him. At 10 a.m. the magistrate took his seat on the bench and the native prisoner was charged before him. 'But this is no offence,' said the magistrate. The police who prosecuted called his attention to the copy of the *Gazette* received an hour before, and the prisoner was punished for an offence of which the magistrate was not himself cognisant!

"During all this time, when a new life was pressing upon him on all sides, made more and more bewildering and complex by the white man, not only in the matter of laws, but as we have seen by the new and irritating conditions in regard to land and labour, his opportunities of approach to those who should have been his fathers, advisers, protectors, were gradually lessened and made more stringent and difficult.

"The native, saturated with his tribal ideas, lacking individualism and initiative, must look to one having these qualities, and upon him he must lean. He cannot stand alone. In the time of Shepstone he looked to him as representing the Government, and felt he had a rock under which he could shelter. But Somtseu had gone, and none had effectively taken his place; the magistrate was busy and the clerks told the rumour-fogged inquirer the 'Nkosi could not attend to him; the road to Pietermaritzburg was closed unless he went through troublesome forms he did not understand. Yet the land was full of rumour, of changes and troubles; and to whom could he go in his bewilderment? Naturally, the white man being utterly inaccessible, he must go to the head of the Black House, the child of Cetywayo.

"The flame was put in the dry grass at Byrne in the midlands of Natal, and spread from Natal by Mapumulo and the Tugela to Zululand. Many lost their lives before it was ended. Indeed it was fortunate it was no worse, and that the lurid light of racial war did not spread over the whole of South Africa."

The Natal Native Commission made their investigation soon after the suppression of the rebellion, and in reference thereto (in Clause 30) they say: "Although the discovery of the cause of the late rebellion is not within the scope of this inquiry, it may be permitted to say they were both material and psychological. It was primarily a revolt against restrictive conditions, assisted by a natural desire, common enough, as history shows, among subject races, to return to their own mode of tribal and family life. All their views of Government, its acts and omissions, benefits and defects, are largely coloured and shaped by the feudalistic traditions of their lives, which, by preventing the development of self-reliance and individual character, has taught them to regard their rulers as the only and natural sources of power, punishment, reward, and welfare. This explains why their attitude towards the Government has been one of alternating expectation and despair. The belief that the conditions they were finding intolerable were attributable in one way or other to Government action or inaction, explains why so little damage was done to private property during the late disturbances. Looking upon Government as the maker and enforcer of laws, the imposer and collector of taxes, the fountain of all authority, with its officers everywhere, they wonder why their family system is allowed to crumble to pieces, and their daughters go astray; why they are compelled through the courts to pay heavy rents and usurious interest; to submit to the overbearing conduct of the police and to laws they were ignorant of, and in the making of which they had no voice. Yet all the time we were flattering ourselves that by giving them peace and a pure justiciary we were doing our whole duty to and by them. We never stopped to think that out system had become too impersonal for the masses or to see the pathos in a simple people looking for fatherly advice and assistance from a purely judicial officer, or longing to consult an exalted and virtually inaccessible Minister. The head of the Native Department had never been approachable by the multitude, while to the chief he was accessible only to a limited extent and in accordance with certain formalities. We live and move and think on different planes, and to make them contented and satisfied with our rule our methods must be less artificial and complicated and nearer the compass of their understanding.

"Is it to be wondered at, then, as the evidence abundantly shows, that the more intelligent and reflective among the natives so frequently drew comparisons between the consideration and treatment shown them in pre-responsible Government days, when the personal factor had sway, and what it is to-day, when this element had been practically eliminated altogether? A system of government that disregards natural laws, and leaves out of account the idiosyncrasy of the people, is doomed to failure."

General Hertzog's Government, within its first twelve months, introduced a greater number of anti-native measures in Parliament than any previous Union Government—not including the four further Bills since proposed which I have examined.

It is complacently taken for granted that this traditional South African attitude towards the native races is natural and legitimate. The native obviously does not share this assumption: his appreciation of the facts of the white man's system as they affect him appear, in marked contrast, to be quite normal and reasonable. His land is taken away from him, his tribal cohesion is broken up, he is tied and bound by labour laws and pass regulations. His feelings about these things are exactly what any intelligent outsider would expect from a white race. They

are perfectly clearly conceived and are expressed
in appropriate, accurate, and unanswerable English
sentences. Mr Evans gives the history of the
Zulu Rebellion, and the causes for it set out by
the natives in the resulting inquiry. The only
judgment possible on the facts is that (as in
Matabeleland also) the self-seeking of the whites
and the gross lack of common intelligence on the
part of the Government was entirely responsible.
Injustices and exactions are enacted with as little
compunction as Antonio feels in spitting on
Shylock, and through a similar overbearingness
of temper and crass mental obtusity. As the
native cannot resist them, he economises his
energies and waits. "Time longer dan Rope."
Equally remarkable appear the lack of insight
and appreciation on the part of a prevailing
majority of South Africans, and even of some
politicians who have attained ministerial office,
as to the real character of the natural forces in
man that they have to deal with, and what the
world outside the boundaries of the Bushveld
has made up its mind about in regard to human
rights. Doubtless it was the recognition of this
deficiency of apprehension that prompted Lord
Milner to try to introduce a leaven of active intelligence into South Africa by importing his
"kindergarten" of bright University Englishmen
(of which the present Dominions Secretary is so
distinguished a scion) to help to staff the Press
and the public service. (Only a Balliol graduate,
probably, would have had such confidence in the

special virtues of that particular type, but, if a mean of human excellence was to be aimed at, an emulsion of Balliol and Boer was perhaps well conceived for the purpose.)

There exist in the literature of South African questions many able and perspicacious books, reports, and commentaries; there are the records and speeches of statesmen (to mention only the dead) such as Mr Jan Hofmeyr, Mr J. X. Merriman, General Botha; there are the living results of an enlightened native policy in the Cape Colony, which recognise the facts, the necessities, and the possibilities of the situation, and the injustices felt in the consciousness of every tribal community and protested by every detribalised native who can say in English what his people feel and think. South Africa has not been dealing for a hundred years with labour and native problems without establishing material for judgments based on experience as to the possible and promising and the unworkable and disastrous methods of attempting their solution. There has been continuous and uninterrupted effort on the part of the school of British statesmanship whose base of action was established in the Cape Colony, and the missionary connection of the European Churches, to follow, in native policy, the simple requirement that they should do justice, love mercy, and walk humbly in their relations with their fellow-children of God. They did not always succeed in doing so, and they made their mistakes. Nor did they always do justice to that section of their own white community which became the Boer peoples. But in the Transkei territories of the Cape Colony, and in the Shepstone policy in Natal, consistent endeavour was made to follow these principles, and foundations were laid for a satisfactory accommodation of rights, interests, needs, and manners of social life between the immigrant Europeans and the natives. And although in this history of experiments, inspired by the fundamental principles of Western white civilisation and feeling, there have been errors and failures, no one who surveys the whole field of South Africa can question that the Cape native policy, and in a less degree the less-developed Natal native policy, have produced the most successful, hopeful, and promising results to be recognised in any sphere of native life in South Africa. The Administrative Reports, the observations of the 1924 delegation of the Empire Parliamentary Association, will convince anyone unacquainted locally with the facts. No one acquainted with them can dispute them.

But the European says: "I have got to live. I have appropriated this country. The land is mine, and I am not going to give any away to natives. I need Kaffir labour. If the natives are to have land, if I restore to them even a fair proportion of what I have appropriated, and on which more than half of them are now working or living on sufferance, they will not labour for me. If I concede them any equality in civil rights, and, more especially, if they are helped to thrive on their land and get prosperous and educated and capable of using political power, they will rule South Africa in their own interests and swamp my civilisation." That has always been the argument urged against doing justice, loving mercy, and walking humbly. It grows by what it feeds on, and demands ever more and more application of that injustice in dealings with land, for which General Botha promised remedy, but which General Hertzog finds cannot be remedied in the manner proposed: it demands more and more binding down of the natives to labour, as General Hertzog's Land Bill proposes to bind him down: more and more unmerciful pressure on the "squatter" and the labour tenant (whose tale of days that Bill would double) more and more assertion of European human superiority and superior right, more disfranchisement and oppression of Asiatics (deliberately imported and solemnly promised equality) with a view to making life in Natal unbearable to them and driving them back to India. This guiding principle— the paramount interest of the white man—has also been tried as a guide of policy, and has progressively demonstrated nothing but its own inherent disastrousness. It has had no success, except where a native tribe has been simply destroyed, as the Bushmen and most of the Hottentots were, or driven away, as the remnants of Bantu tribes have been. Where the native has not been eliminated, he increasingly, and necessarily under this policy, produces "the native problem." Alarmed at the imminent prospect of the aggravation of that problem by increase of numbers, the mentality of the repressionist politicians can only conceive demands for a further turn of the screw.

CHAPTER XIX

THE FIVE FEARS OF SOUTH AFRICA

SOUTH AFRICA'S complacency about her "peculiar institution," the "Kaffir boy," has lately been getting disturbed by the notion of what is talked about as the "swamping" of white civilisation. This scare was started largely by the forecasts as to the rapid multiplication of natives made by Mr Cousins in his Report on the census of 1921. Mr Cousins' conclusions are considered by Dr Loram and some other South African publicists to be not entirely convincing as to the probable relative rates of increase of white and black. But, assuming only the indisputably apparent probabilities, what, in brief, is the character of the fears they are provoking?

First, and immediately at the present time, the incentive of the new colour bar legislation is fear of the increasing competition of natives with Europeans in the wage-labour market. This cause of anxiety is not a necessary element in the relations between Europeans and natives inhabiting the same country. It is entirely, here as elsewhere, an incident of the introduction of the capitalist system of industry and exploitation, creating a competitive market for hired labour. It would not exist if white and black were living side by side, either in segregation (if that were possible) or in the more patriarchal relations which long obtained in the agricultural and pastoral industries when the two races remained on the footing of a definite distinction of white man and Kaffir, master and bonded servant. In so far as it is an incident of competition for wages in a labour market, it is amenable and can be made amenable only to the same methods of dealing with such problems of industry under the capitalist system as are being worked out in other capitalist industrial societies. In that aspect the problem is exhaustively and convincingly handled in the Reports of the Economic Commission. Even if those Reports may appear to leave unsolved some problems which may imaginably arise in the future as the population increases, they are so cogent and so adequate as regards immediate questions, and already so far in advance of the ideas at present accepted among the majority of the South African electorate, that it would be idle and tedious for me to repeat them. I can only wish them a widening influence and acceptance. The alternative empirical prescription of the colour bar, which they entirely condemn, could only have any curative effect on South African malady if the industries in which it is demanded that it should be applied could be entirely worked without natives, and the natives restored to the position of being able to support themselves upon adequate land and in a system of industry subserving their own needs alone. Such segregation, even in Rhodesia, is impossible, and is not desired by white men.

In a second aspect the fear of an increase of natives arises from a bad conscience. The injustice and lack of consideration with which the natives have been dealt with in regard to land, the declaration of war against Africans involved in the Colour Bar Law, and the obstinate unintelligence and presumption of the attitude of traditional Afrikander social theory in respect of them, are all exasperating elements producing good reason for fear of increasing native resentment. But native resentment by itself some white men appear to think they can afford to ignore for the present, and so thinking they will support General Hertzog's native policy. They believe that the white man's weapons can always repress native rebellion. That, however, is not a kind of security which will permanently enable the white man to "remain and to rule" in Africa, if only because, as the Transvaal farmer quoted by Dr Jabavu observed, there are some things in the pursuit of repression which cannot be done by Europeans to natives, more especially when the reason for resorting to acts of repression arises from the white man's own injustice. The Portuguese methods of destroying and disheartening the African native are still repugnant to influential European feeling in the Union.

Quite apart from the probable influence of this truth and of sane and intelligent South Africans in raising the level of their community's understanding and temper, civilised Europe and America might have a good deal to say on a policy of white terrorism. That world does not easily recognise the high quality of a white civilisation which exhibits such characteristics as those illustrated by the quotations which I have made from the memoirs of the ingenuous Mr De Waal, in which we were shown the Prime Minister of the Cape Colony and his fellow members of the Legislative Assembly pommelling and "severely thrashing" unoffending and faithful servants without the least provocation, and threatening them with flogging because a portmanteau was torn on a journey and a palm-nut had fallen out. When some of the Boer War prisoners interned in Ceylon assumed, as quite natural and legitimate, in their relations with the dark-skinned people of that British Colony, the standards of behaviour displayed by Mr Rhodes and his friends, they provoked some nasty retaliations; and there would, doubtless, soon be provoked rather dangerous reactions in Africa on the part of the natives if these were to cease to hope that by patience they and British standards of civilisation may live down these traditions of slavedom. Unless the slave doctrine of "Kaffir work" and status is outgrown in South Africa, as the Economic Commission tell us it does show signs of being outgrown, and unless concurrently with that growth equality of consideration is recognised as the due of all those who are doing similar service, that patience will in course of time be wearied out.

The increasing arrogance and insolence of detribalised and urbanised natives is frequently now complained of. They are, it is said, ceasing to respect the whites. At any rate they are ceasing to behave as if they respected them. That, in so far as it is the result of closer observation and contact, not only may be very natural and indeed inevitable—for no South African native could reasonably respect the Poor Whites, any more than the American negro could respect the "white trash" of the Southern States—but is in a great measure creditable to their standards of human judgment, and of good omen for the future of the mixed community of South Africa. But apart from the phenomenon of the Poor White it is questionable whether the ideals and morals of triumphant European civilisation as exhibited, for example, in Johannesburg, to say nothing of its eclectic delights and interests as advertised to the world through the moving pictures—a very popular entertainment with urban Africans everywhere—could reasonably or desirably be expected to enhance the respect of the natives for white people. If the native had not sufficient sense of dignity and decency to despise a great deal in European civilisation, in proportion as the ostensibly typical characteristics of its well-to-do classes are more and more pressed on his notice, the prospects of the future of South Africa and of any similar mixed community might well appear more ominous than they actually are, or need be, if the white man will safeguard his own standard of dignity, decency, and good taste. When the European emperor really is naked, the native, not having been trained to accept the Court convention that he is faultlessly clothed, will, in all simplicity, lewdly deride his figure.

In the third place, South Africans fear that white civilisation may be infected, or the morale of its European stocks deteriorated by the mere induction of the proximity of increasing numbers of natives, and that the white man may adopt Kaffir habits. If there is danger of this, the only two conceivable methods for averting it, true segregation being neither possible nor desired, would be either resolutely to kill off the native increase year by year, and establish the white man in the position formerly held by the Matabele among the Mashonas, which would not be a preservation of white civilisation, or to take steps to ensure that the encroaching black population shall be increasingly civilised. White people in contact with backward races are demoralised and deteriorated just in proportion to their own inferiority to the normal white standard, and, concurrently, in proportion to the degradation and barbarism of the population with which they consort. On the other hand it is proved that continuous contact, intermixture, and admission to the utilities of white civilisation attract and slowly but surely raise the standard of a black population. It is proved by experience in the United States and in the West Indies, and obviously in some measure in South Africa, and even if the results of experience and the special conditions of racial contact in South Africa, where uncivilised natives are proportionately more numerous than in the United States, do not encourage the hope that such advance can be then very rapid. It is the only line of advance towards greater security that exists to be looked to. One apparent difficulty is that it is questionable whether South African whites are prepared to prove themselves capable of working that line.

The one conspicuous general example of degeneration in the white race and its civilisation in South Africa is the case of the Poor White. And that has not been due to contact with native tribalism or to the preponderance in numbers of black over white. It is common ground with all who concern themselves with interracial relations that the conditions of European town life are disastrously demoralising to the native, and that city life in such conditions of contact with natives is reciprocally, but certainly in a less marked degree, demoralising to whites. But their demoralisation is not greater than it is in European city slums or even in less indigent spheres of society where there is no contact with black races. It is not this degree of white demoralisation that is regarded as presaging a menace to European civilisation in South Africa through an increasing proportion of natives. If it were, the simple and straightforward prescription for that evil is obvious. Keep the native out of the cities by allowing him to have land on which he can live a life more natural and wholesome for him. It is entirely the pressure and policy of the European, which General Hertzog's land programme will reinforce, that drives or attracts him to the cities.

The Poor White is a disease of rural white Afrikanderism—a characteristic product of that section of South African society that has kept itself most aloof from natives. Professor Duerden of Grahamstown College, in his Presidential address (1921) to the South African Association for the Advancement of Science, on "Social Anthropology in South Africa," analysed the conditions which have produced the degeneration of the fine European stock into the Poor Whites, and points out, as the Economic and Wages Commission have done, the only conditions for arresting this degradation. He attributes it, independently of the subdivision of land which I already mentioned, to isolation, lack of education, easygoing and slovenly habits of farming, in conditions in which a mere livelihood was easy and there was abundance of leisure, and dependence on the native for manual work. He recognises, as do the Economic Commissioners, that the prejudice against Kaffir work is being modified. "There is," he says, "some reason to hope that the indigent white will insensibly disappear as a special class. . . . If given a new start, all but those inefficient by nature should recover, and the rising generation may be retrieved. The new

agricultural and industrial development of South
Africa carries with it the call for this regenerated
class. Everywhere is the growing demand for
efficient whites. Farmers demand efficient whites
for their intensive agriculture and high pastoral
attainments, industrialism calls for a high level of
production only possible from efficients."

It was not therefore any contact with or influence of Bantu native life that produced the Poor
White class, except in so far as its inefficiency,
indolence, and idleness were fostered and stereotyped by the South African slave-state doctrine
that work was only for Kaffirs; nor is it such
contact or influence that maintains or can aggravate it, except in so far as that slave-state doctrine
is clung to. Nothing is more astonishing in
the contemporary operation of South African
politics than that whereas the causes which have
produced the "poor white" have been perfectly
clearly recognised, and a sane policy in regard to
that problem actually adopted, and in some degree
put into operation by the Union Government,
General Hertzog should, in order to please his
farmer-employer constituents, or, on the most
charitable presumption, because he believes it to
be good for the native, propose to undercut
the whole agricultural terrain indicated by Professor Duerden as affording hope for the rescue
of the Poor White class, by forcing into employment on the farms, at Kaffir wages, under the
Masters and Servants Laws, an enormous flood
of natives, to be expelled from the position of

squatters by the operation of his Natives Land
Act Amendment Law.

The only hope for reinstating the Poor White
as a producer in agriculture is to withdraw from
the employing farmer this forced supply of native
labour and to place it in a position to improve
its own standard of living, whilst at the same time
making it worth while for the farmer, if white
labour is really more efficient than black, to pay
it a living wage, and also compelling the Poor
White, if he is replaced on the land, to learn to
do his own work and not to rely upon Kaffir
labour. Nothing can be more demoralising for
such white men as through weakness of character
are in danger of deterioration by contact with
natives (and no doubt such danger exists), than
that they should live in association with natives
on the basis of the racial assumptions still persistent in South Africa, ostentatiously reinforced
by the industrial colour bar policy which seeks
to stereotype those disastrous fallacies.

In many cases there is not the slightest reason
for regarding a particular white man, on any
schedule of human values, as superior to a black.
In many cases white men are quite obviously
less desirable as contributors to the future of the
world, and even of the South African State, than
many black men. Most white men of intelligence and sensibility who have had, in favour-
able conditions, opportunities of intercourse with
Africans are aware that there is much of essentially
human character and faculty that is habitually

better realised in the superior African and even in the average African than it is in the average European. These faculties must be preserved and may make valuable contribution to the human societies of the future. But Professor Duerden, who has had experience of, and contact with, black and coloured races in various parts of the world, recognises very clearly the truth on which I have already insisted, namely, that the European is a very much more advanced and efficient human type than the native African, and that therefore he "must" for long, by the mere force of his acquired qualities, continue to maintain his social supremacy in South Africa, and need not be afraid of increasing numbers of natives, provided he does not demoralise himself as the progenitors of the Poor Whites demoralised their offspring—by adherence to those ideas about natives and about the modes in which an industrial society can afford to deal with them which I have criticised in this Anatomy.

If too great a number of natives is a menace to white civilisation, it might be thought strange that eighty or ninety thousand should be imported from Portuguese East Africa every year. But these, being kept locked up in the mine compounds, are presumably deemed incapable of doing much swamping. And the nearest approach to the discipline of the compounds that can be applied to the rural native is to get him bound to a farmer under the Masters and Servants Law as General Hertzog's new Land Bill aims at doing for him. But this will only increase the redundancy of those that cannot be so placed.

South African European society displays a strong antagonism to interracial conjugal unions. The fear of increasing miscegenation may be mentioned as a fourth factor contributing to the apprehension with which the increase in the proportion of natives in the population is contemplated. But there is really no adequate reason for supposing that such mere increase of numbers is likely to promote that result. In the matter of interracial unions, as in various others in which public opinion and policy are mobilised against the native, whatever evil exists is the result of the inclinations and actions of Europeans themselves, and its mitigations depend upon white men's or white women's control of their own behaviour. The continual increase in the numerical preponderance of black and coloured persons over white in the West Indies has been accompanied not by an increase, but by a decrease in the amount of illicit intimacy between white men and black or coloured women in proportion to their respective numbers. The easy complaisance of women of African race whose traditional controls have been entirely (as in the West Indies and America) or partially, as in detribalised South Africa, destroyed, towards the desires of equally uncontrolled white men is no doubt a continual source of temptation and sexual licence to white men, living among detribalised

Africans, who in a purely European society would have adhered more consistently to the ostensible, if not actually very strictly observed, European moral standards. But the extent of such demoralisation has no dependence on the relative gross numbers of the two races; it depends upon the circumstances in which Europeans live among Africans: where, for example, the alternatives for a young white man are either celibacy or association with black, or coloured, women. The trekking Boers, isolated from opportunity, and by universal juvenile marriages avoided such relations; but the early marriages and very large families of the Boers have resulted in a progeny of Poor Whites which is a more undesirable element in the South African population than are the coloured people begotten by their own progenitors before they quitted the Cape. Many white men cannot, and will not, marry into such prospects. Intermarriage or illicit relations between descendants of the different races there will, it may be taken as certain, continue to be. They are not eliminated by the colour bar and the legislation against intermarriage in the United States. But interbreeding has always been most rife where the two races have been in the positions of master and slave respectively, or where low-class white men have been in contact with coloured peoples whose own systems for the control of their women have been destroyed, as it has always been a complaint of the tribal Bantus and also of other native peoples that the European destroys them. Racial intermixture may or may not be destined to increase in South Africa. Whether in all its ultimate outcomes it is a good or an evil thing that it should occur is a disputable question. Anyhow, the coloured people are there, nearly one-third as many in number as the whites. At the present time, so far as South Africa is concerned, it may be accepted as a sufficiently conclusive fact that dominant social feeling condemns miscegenation and that neither race desires it.

The House of Assembly has even attempted legislation on the fringe of this matter, by passing (last April) a Bill to prohibit, under penalty of whipping, illicit intercourse between European males and native women; also solicitation on the part of either, procuration of native women for immoral purposes or connivance by the owner or occupier of premises where such offences may occur. This measure, well intentioned in its ostensible, if limited purpose, so far as it goes, has been ill-naturedly alleged to be designed as a pendant, in protection of female industry in Johannesburg and the seaport towns, to the Colour Bar Law conceded to the white and the franchise proposed to be given to the coloured man. Prostitution is not, in fact, an indigenous trade among native women, but it is becoming prevalent in the towns, and habitual competition of native with white and coloured women in that market might doubtless become as annoying to them as native male competition to the skilled white worker.

The social relations which the pursuit of the repressionist policy, combined with the continued intermixture of white and coloured people in every department of life, must inevitably tend to produce, will not extinguish interracial unions. Experience both in the United States and in the West Indies shows that irregular interbreeding in such communities tends to diminish only as both races raise themselves out of the mentality of the servile state which at present so largely dominates South African white society. Honourable relations between men and women of whatever race are determined by perfectly well-understood considerations and instincts of personal and human dignity, and no social policy which does not accept the necessity of recognising similar human standards for both the races can do anything to promote that common understanding and mutual respect.

The fifth form of the fear of increasing numbers prompts the argument that the native must not be given equal rights of political franchise or Parliamentary representation. It has not been this book's purpose to discuss expediencies in the structure of the political Constitution, but to exhibit special causes which do in fact contribute to make the question of the admission to political franchise specially difficult in South Africa. I think it very much more important that the community should reform its ideas and pursue a sane policy in the sphere of its economic and social institutions and theories than that it should tinker with the existing political franchise at all. General Hertzog's Government has, however, tabled certain proposals, based apparently on severely logical arguing, on which in so far as they do bear on the topics I have been discussing I must make some very brief observations. The arguments appear to be somewhat as follow. If all South African natives had the Parliamentary vote, or representation in Parliament, South Africa would be governed by black men and not by white. In my judgment, it is for reasons I have explained, not in the least degree probable that it would be, but it is dialectically arguable that such must be the ultimate outcome if every native has the vote and uses it in his own racial interests: and if he will not, what is the purpose of giving it to him? But granting this, as I believe, fallacious hypothesis, it is obvious that the franchise cannot be extended if white men exclusively are to rule; and whether it is necessary that white men exclusively should rule or not, they have at present the power to extend or curtail the franchise as they think best.

As then on this hypothesis natives outside the Cape Province cannot be given the franchise, the natives, it is argued, within that Province must be deprived of it. That, logical as it may appear, does not in the least degree follow. In the first place, because the native franchise there does not swamp and shows no symptoms of being likely to swamp European civilisation—and would not be likely to do so even if all the natives used their votes, so long as Europeans do not force them into that consolidation of race-opposition which the colour bar and repression policies seek to do, aggravating the existing maladies inherited from the slave period and intensified by capitalism. Liberal ideas in the Cape have in the past wholesomely neutralised these tendencies in the sphere of politics, but the withdrawal of such existing privileges would be a provocative imbecility which no far-seeing statesman would dream of proposing. The theoretical illogicality of maintaining the present discrimination between the Provinces would be a far lesser political imprudence: to say nothing of the established rights of Cape natives.

The privilege of registration can only be withdrawn from them by a two-thirds vote of the Senate and House of Assembly together. Those who have the vote cannot be removed from the register without a breach of the Constitution established in the South Africa Act, which preserves their rights.

Further, on grounds of logic, because General Hertzog does not think it wise to disfranchise the Cape coloured people, he proposes to enfranchise coloured men in the other Provinces: and recruit them partially to the side of the white community. Partially only, because they are to have special communal representation.

The Bills introduce the stupid and pernicious

principle, which has proved so disastrous in India, of communal representation, and will, if adopted, establish in Parliament a solid block of votes representing native interests only, whereas the native vote in the Cape has never resulted in any such sectional representation.

These proposals involve setting up definitions of what is a native and what is a coloured person, and two new colour bar tests have to be devised. Of the elaborate and complicated principles of discrimination proposed in the Bills, it is sufficient to say that they are frankly preposterous, illogical, and absurd, and contemplate lines of distinction between coloured and white, and native and coloured which are completely arbitrary, and would include in each community persons preponderantly of the blood of the other, and exclude from each persons preponderantly of its own origin. The tests themselves and the machinery for applying them would be set an impossible task. It remains to be seen whether South African white legislators will stultify themselves by adopting them.

NOTE

"To assume that in this day of the training of *peoples*, of the development and equipment, not merely of a selected leadership, but of human aggregates, we can ever measurably succeed upon a labour basis of crude 'untrained muscle,' of mere stolid, stupid animal power, is to forget that elementary truth which throughout our discussion has seemed to appear and reappear in many forms —the truth that whenever a social group persistently maintains, in relation to an included group, a policy of constriction and repression, there follows the constriction and repression of its own life. Not only is it embarrassed and constrained by the actual loss of the energies and capacities which it restricts, but the reactive force of its restrictive policies—absorbing its mind in the preoccupations of constraint—confines and hardens the largeness of its own temper, the varied fertility of its own thinking, the scope and freedom of its development. To be long busied with the task of holding a labourer by the throat is an engrossing, confining, oppressive occupation —not to the labourer alone."—Edgar Gardner Murphy, *The Basis of Ascendancy.* Longmans. 1910.

CHAPTER XX

CONCLUSIONS

THE immediate provocation to the writing of this Anatomy has been the new departure of the South African Government, unique in the history of civilised peoples, in importing the principle of the colour bar into the industrial law of a state heretofore based on the Christian and British Imperial theory of equal human rights. That declaration is a menace to the peace of the world. I have exhibited, using the materials abundantly collected and set forth by South Africans, what are the causes and the significance of this disquieting new departure. The basic cause is that the South African community has never assimilated the principle in application of which the British and American communities decreed the abolition of slavery, and I have pointed out that the social relations thus preserved were reinforced and stereotyped by the intrusion of the capitalist system of industry into South Africa, established, especially in regard to the vast enterprise of the mining industry, on the basis of the theory of Kaffir work and Kaffir pay. The importance of the mining industry makes it extraordinarily difficult, economically, for the community to get away from its dependence upon that theory, even

227

upon the lines so sanely advised by the Economic and Wages Commission. It is also a deplorable fact that the theory appears to have infected and corrupted the South African Labour Party into the acceptance of a programme which is absolutely and explicitly condemned by the formulated programme of the British Labour Party in regard to relations with native races. That Party demands, as the Economic Commission demand, the allowance of equal opportunities to all men of equal qualifications, the standardisation of wages at adequate minimum levels, and the development of the policy, already supported by all the most intelligent opinion in South Africa, of native education. Concurrently with these industrial and educational demands it insists—and by no means more forcibly than South African statesmen have themselves insisted—upon the necessity for providing the native with sufficient land, which the policy of the present South African Government does not promise effectually to do, whereas in the contrary direction it aims at turning natives off land which they are still occupying by sufferance of its white appropriators and forcing them into bonded employment with the farmers or to seek jobs in the towns. I have pointed out how the diffusion of the evil principles of slave-theory and capitalist exploitation spread infection through Rhodesia and into Kenya, out of which communities there is some grounds for hope that they are being slowly driven back. Unless the British Government desires to be associated with the encouragement of those dangers to civilisation and world peace which the pursuit of the present policy of the Government of South Africa involves, it will not concede a further inch of administrative authority to that Government in South Africa; and it must resolutely maintain the repudiation of those principles which have already grown up in Rhodesia and have, after a protracted struggle, been recently asserted in Kenya.

No one framing a judgment about South African public opinion and native questions from the latest formulations of Government policy would gather that there prevails to-day, any more than when Mr Maurice Evans wrote, seventeen years ago, what I have quoted in a former chapter, any general and effective recognition that anything requires modification in the accepted assumptions as to the proper economic position of the native, or as to the right of the European to have dealt as he has done with most of the land of the country. Such a judgment, however, would be widely erroneous. There is and has been continuous protest against the attitude now dominant, and it has had some continuous effect. Recognition of what is needed is growing, but it is not yet general: it is not yet politically effective. It has, in fact, become comparatively less politically effective during the last few years than it was fifty years ago; when it was possible to lay down liberally conceived native policies in Natal and the Cape Province. Repression is not a policy, and that is all that the strongest political combination in the Union apparently now stands for.

It is something, however, to find even a Nationalist representative of a Northern Province talking in the Assembly about "our Western civilisation," even when he was urging, on the Defence Vote, increase of the provision for commandos in view of the "internal dangers that threaten," in his opinion, that civilisation. South Africans may presently come to apprehend more generally what the said standards imply, and that the views which they themselves still hold about native Africans, and the principles on which they are still trying to deal with them, are not those of Western or European or Christian civilisation. But that "Western standards" should have come to be spoken of as valid is at least a hopeful symptom, and is possibly one of the fruits of South African Union. There are plenty of South Africans who can continue to influence their fellow-citizens towards recognition of where the value and the power of those standards really lie, and of how little white commandos can avail to maintain them. But all South Africa is still practically dominated and her future endangered by the persistence of the same slave-state mind and practice, elimination of which is one of the most important things that Western civilisation primarily stands for.

Many leading South African statesmen and commentators on public affairs have for years past been aware of and disquieted about the facts of the situation, and have recognised its causes, as I have exhibited them, and the character of the necessary remedies. The war delayed attention to them, and after the war the deaths of 500,000 natives from influenza and the associated depression of native vitality for a time checked the increasing pressure of native populations against the boundaries of their maintenance and the restrictions of their freedom.

Writing on White Capital and Coloured Labour in South Africa in 1905, in the light of the Report of the South African Native Affairs Commission published that year, I found the facts underlying the situation almost as clear then as they are to-day; but I did not then so clearly apprehend their history. More recent Commissions and South African commentators have realised and exhibited the facts and their causes more clearly and thoroughly than did the Commission of 1903–5, and it is interesting to compare the degrees of their apprehension and the clarification of their suggestions of policy. The last—the Report of the Economic Commission—even limited as it is by its regard to the conditions of practical politics, is the most perspicacious within its scope and the most obviously and convincingly sound in its advice. But the politicians—or perhaps it would be fairer to say the majority of the white voters who elect them—appear, to judge from their projects of policy, to be able to learn nothing.

If the attempt to maintain the repressionist

and colour bar policy is persisted in, it is not the natives that in the long run are likely to be defeated. It is not they, but the whites, that have shown the first symptoms of degeneration—a degeneration entirely due to their own perverse social theory. The native remains robust and virile, he can live on much less than the European, he increases faster in numbers. He is at present desirous and disposed to adapt himself to the life of the European community: and if white men worthy of their own civilisation continue to endeavour to assist him to do so, South African society will develop on stable lines. Those who know and understand the native best, and those of his own race who can handle the ideas of Western enlightenment, are perfectly clear that although his patience is long, it is not likely to prove eternal in the face of the repressionist policy of which the Colour Bar Law is so outspoken a declaration.

NOTE

IT has not been part of the scheme of this book to vindicate the human capacities of African native peoples against the ignorant lack of appreciation still largely prevalent among white people. I expressed my own observations on that topic in *White Capital and Coloured Labour*, and had only thought it necessary in this book to advert to it in the Chapters on "Afrikander Provincialism" (XVIII), and "The Five Fears of South Africa" (XIX). Here, however, are three brief recent testimonies:—

"I have listened to thousands of old native men of many different tribes in my time, I have heard them speak their inmost thoughts, not through interpreters—who ever learned anything through an interpreter? I have studied these people in and out of Court, officially and privately, in their kraals and in the veld during many years, and I say that I can find nothing whatever throughout the whole gamut of the native's conscious life and soul to differentiate him from other human beings in other parts of the world."—PIETER NIELSON, *The Black Man's Place in South Africa*. 1922. Quoted by MR EDWIN J. SMITH in *The Golden Stool*. 1926.

THE ANATOMY OF AFRICAN MISERY

"Speaking with his wide experience as a judge, SIR THOMAS GRAHAM said that he had formed the definite conviction that there was no substantial difference in natural ability between the White and the Black. . . ."—W. H. DAWSON, South Africa. 1925.

"Great as may be the glamour of the land, it is as nothing to that of the men and women who live there. . . . *Men who have travelled all round the earth say that these Central Africans are the most attractive humans they have seen on the earth.*" —DR DONALD FRASER of Nyasaland, in a "broadcast" talk on Missionary Work in Central Africa. December 1926.